D1118522

ACT NOW!

By Dale L. Anderson, M.D.

Successful Acting Techniques You Can Use Everyday to Dramatically Improve Health, Wealth, and Relationships

CHRONIMED PUBLISHING

Library of Congress Cataloging-in-Publication Data

Anderson, Dale L., M.D.

Act Now! Successful Acting Techniques You Can Use Everyday to Dramatically Improve Health, Wealth, and Relationships. / Dale L. Anderson, M.D.

Includes index
ISBN 1-56561-067-0;
$11.95

Edited by: Doug Toft
Managing Editor: Donna Hoel
Cover Design: Emerson, Wajdowicz Studios Inc./NYC
Text Design/Production: Janet Hogge
Production Manager: Claire Lewis
Printed in the United States of America

Published by
Chronimed Publishing
P.O. Box 59032
Minneapolis, MN 55459-9686

• •

DEDICATION

This book is dedicated to my parents, Francis and Irene Anderson, who were the most significant producers and directors of my genetic, social, and emotional performance.

As role models they set the stage and provided a script that said,

> *"Life is a gift, a gift to be cherished and enjoyed.*
> *A gift to be lovingly shared with others.*
> *A gift that is meaningful, valuable, and FUN."*

ACKNOWLEDGMENTS

Special thanks to:

- The dedicated and professional staff of Chronimed Publishing.

- The more than 400 physician colleagues and 2,000 support staff of Park Nicollet Clinic–Health Systems Minnesota for fostering a medical environment that encourages physician individuality, innovation, and entrepreneurship. I appreciate the group's commitment to the highest standards and its constant striving to improve the delivery and quality of health care.

- The Complementary Care Department and Complementary Care Study groups of Park Nicollet Clinic, who are open to finding the good in alternative medicine and integrating into medical practice those aspects that enhance patients' satisfaction and well-being.

- The Park Nicollet Medical Foundation for encouraging the development of "edu-taining" SHAPE lifestyle programs.

- The platform friends of the National Speakers Association for setting high standards and providing inspiration to strive toward and achieve excellence.

- Douglas Toft for his organizational, writing, and editorial expertise.

- The valued teachers, friends, and physician colleagues who over the years helped me "right" and "re-right" my script.

- The thousands of wonderful patients who, during my physician career, have cared for me while I cared for them.

- My wife Barbara, sons Lance, Shane, and Chad and their families.

- And YOU, the reader—a new star is born.

TABLE OF CONTENTS

FOREWORD

You can take several different paths through *Act Now:* One, of course, is to read the contents straight through, in their given order. Another option is to read the Prologue and then go directly to Chapters 4 through 10 to get immediate suggestions.

Note that chapter 3 goes into acting techniques (specifically Stanislavski's "Method") in some detail. You might wish to skim this chapter at first and come back to it later for a more careful reading.

Writing a manuscript that's gender-fair is a constant issue for authors. To give *Act Now* an inclusive tone, I've alternated randomly between male and female pronouns.

ACT NOW!

· ·

· ·

PROLOGUE

IN AND OUT OF THE "PSYCH" WARD

In the early 1970s, David Reynolds, an anthropologist and faculty member at the University of Southern California, grew fascinated by the question of how to prevent suicide among clinically depressed people. He wanted to find out how such people were treated when they entered mental wards, what triggered their thoughts of suicide, what helped them, and what hurt them.

At his disposal were all the conventional, respected methods for doing this kind of research: interviewing hospital staff members and patients, observing group therapy, reading medical records and journals, administering psychological tests, and the like. Reynolds planned to use several of these methods. Even so, none of these would tell him precisely what he wanted to know—how it felt to move through the halls of a mental ward and pass the days there as an insider. That left only one choice: Reynolds would have to *become* a mental patient.

 **ACT NOW!**

To do that, he literally transformed himself. Like an actor preparing to play a scene from *One Flew Over the Cuckoo's Nest* or *Marat/Sade*, this skilled and respected researcher developed his role and memorized his lines. Within days Reynolds became a man so profoundly depressed that he was immediately placed on "SOS" (suicide observation status) during his stay at a VA hospital.

Reynolds even altered his official biography and changed his name for the purposes of this research project. In a matter of a few days, the real David Kent Reynolds, anthropologist and professor, became "David Kent," a suicidally depressed patient in a California VA hospital. Reynolds acted the part so well that his true identity was never suspected—not even by the psychologists, psychiatrists, nurses, and other professionals who worked at the hospital.

How did he do it? Writing about the experience later, Reynolds explained:

> I had to learn how to make myself depressed—an unusual task, to be sure. . . . Depression can be created by sitting slouched in a chair, shoulders hunched, head hanging down. Repeat these words over and over: "There's nothing I can do. No one can help me. It's hopeless. I'm helpless. I give up." Shake your head, sigh, cry. In general, act depressed and the genuine feeling will follow in time.

Becoming David Kent, a suicidally depressed patient, was only half of his task. The other half was returning to the outside world when his hospital stay was over and resuming his role as a teacher and writer. Once again this anthropologist became an actor, transforming himself from David Kent back to the more healthy, true self, David Reynolds. That meant using many of the same acting strategies in reverse.

First, Kent had to become physically active, even though he didn't feel like it. Try sitting down for a whole day and see what it does to your mood (not to mention your intestinal tract). Brisk walks, tennis, and jogging helped. Increased stimulus of all sorts was necessary. Cheery music and bright colors made a difference. It also helped to interact with friends who knew his healthy identity and expected him to be active and alert. Fresh scenery and fresh clothes helped mark the change.

During his hospital stay, Reynolds kept a detailed journal—writings that formed the basis for two subsequent books, *Suicide Inside Out* and *Endangered Hope*. These volumes combined first-hand accounts of his experiences as a mental patient with academic analysis and a list of recommendations for hospitals that treat depressed people.

Here's the point

Why dwell at length on Reynolds' various transformations? Because they illustrate the main point of *Act Now*. Drawing from the tradition of the theater, we can create a new way to think about health.

This way of thinking is based on the idea that we become what we do. In short, we could become more healthy by acting like healthy people. Modern science supports an old intuition: that when we "get our act together," our physiology also improves. I offer this idea not as a proven fact but as a perspective that's worth considering and applying.

Like David Kent, many of us are playing parts that work against our ideal of healthy, vibrant living. By acting instead the parts of happy, healthy people (as David *Reynolds* did in leaving the mental ward), we may be able to trigger lasting change in ourselves.

The physical and emotional changes we induce by acting different roles may even register at the very level of our cells. Among these are changes in the levels of chemicals that bolster the human immune system and promote well-being. Two recent studies bring this idea home to me with special force. Both point to a connection between health and acting that we cannot afford to ignore.

Multiple personalities, multiple immune systems

The first study appeared in the fall 1994 edition of *Advances: The Journal of Mind-Body Health*. The article, titled "Transformation of Personality and the Immune System," detailed a collaboration between the fields of theater and medicine.

Representing medicine were Nicolas Hall and Maureen O'Grady, both faculty members in the Department of Psychiatry and Behavioral Medicine at the University of South Florida. They were joined by Denis Calandra, chairman of the Department of Theater at the University.

Hall and his colleagues had already made ventures into the topic of mind-body connections. One of their projects involved the study of people with multiple personalities. Their question was this: Would the different personalities who "resided" in these people have different immune systems as well?

Accept for the moment that thoughts and feelings can affect a person's ability to maintain health and resist disease. What would happen to a person's immune system, then, if this person switched personalities?

Hall and his colleagues did find variations in the immune function that seemed to vary with personality. Working with the National Institute of Mental Health, Hall's team began by observing a woman with multiple personality disorder. This woman, in fact, claimed to have more than 200 different personalities. Their ages ranged from 2 to 90; their races were Caucasian, native American, and African American; their genders were both male and female. And all of these personalities resided in the body of a 32-year-old woman.

Not surprisingly, the research team ran into logistical problems almost from the start. First was the issue of consent. If you work with someone who has many personalities, then which personality do you ask for consent to take part in a study? Some of this woman's personalities, remember, were underage. (One personality even appeared to be nonhuman—that of an animal.) Initially the researchers got around this problem by communicating with a host personality—one who seemed to predominate.

At that point, the research team was ready for business. Working with Dr. Frank Putnam, a psychiatrist who knew the woman, researchers invited four of her personalities to appear. Each personality was present for a half hour. In addition, researchers took a sample of the woman's blood whenever a new personality came to the surface. In fact, two of her blood samples were taken within 30 to 40 seconds of each other—the time between the end of one personality's sample and the beginning of the next.

After the "interview" with these four personalities, laboratory technicians ran some tests on the respective blood samples. One test measured the number of times that lymphocytes (a type of blood cell) could divide.

Lymphocytes are a key element of the human immune system, and their ability to divide is crucial to protecting the body from disease. When a virus or bacteria enters the body, an army of lymphocytes launches to fend off this invader. Each time a lymphocyte divides, it offers more recruits for the defending army. Measuring how often this division takes place, then, is one way to look at how well a person's immune system is working.

Now the researchers had some precise numbers to work with. And they *did* observe a large amount of variability between the personalities and their immune responses. In other words, the different personalities showed different potentials for health and disease.

Writing about this study for *Advances*, Hall and his colleagues reported that they decided to give up this line of research. "For one," noted Hall, "it is rare to find someone who can actually control their personalities as could the subject I have just described. We also ran into a legal problem with this subject, in that the host personality changed and threatened to sue us if we did anything with the data."

Add to this another difficulty. Hall could not be sure whether this woman was only pretending to display different personalities. Dr. Putnam was present during the interview to verify that the personalities that appeared were genuinely different from a clinical standpoint. Even so, the question remained: Were the multiple personalities an act?

"In a sense, it really didn't matter," Hall wrote. "Acting or not, we had already observed variability with respect to the immune system measures we chose to assess."

Yet this issue took on a life of its own. Hall and his fellow researchers asked the next logical question: Why not perform a similar study with clinically normal people who have professional experience taking on different personalities—that is, actors?

Hall's next study grew directly from that question. This time, the researchers involved two members of the University of South

Florida's theater department. Hall and his colleagues gave these actors two plays to perform. One was a comedy—a script from an old episode of the *I Love Lucy* television series. The other was a drama by Peter Barnes, titled *It's Cold, Wanderer, It's Cold*; its tone, in Hall's words, was "one of depression." These plays were specifically chosen to present each actor with two markedly different roles.

The format of this study was similar to that of the multiple personality study. Researchers took blood samples from each actor at many points—before rehearsal, during rehearsal, and during several performances conducted at the same time each day over two weeks. Again, researchers measured the amount of division in the actors' lymphocytes. They performed other measures of immune function as well.

Hall explains the study results:

> The data suggested that there was a correlation between the type of personality being performed and immune responsiveness. The female performer exhibited an elevated rate of . . . lymphocyte cell division after the comedy, and a decrease after the drama. . . . Similarly, the male performer exhibited comparable changes consistent with the personality being performed.

Actors alter their chemistry

Results like these are less surprising when we remember something about the nature of emotion: Feelings are chemicals, and chemicals are feelings.

When you're feeling happy, optimistic, energized, or productive, your body chemistry is different than when you're feeling sad,

ACT NOW!

pessimistic, tired, or defeated. I'll say more about this in scene 1, which explores the findings of psychoneuroimmunology, the new science of mind-body connections. At this point I'll simply offer an idea for you to consider: Feelings are chemicals, and chemicals can be changed by acting. Exploring the many facets of this idea is the purpose of this book.

Acting techniques, after all, are strategies to get us moving, speaking, and thinking in different ways. Changes in our movement, speech, and thinking can lead to changes in our feelings.

As a physician, my job is to help people improve their level of health. From a scientific basis, this has often led me to treat disease through surgery, medications, and recommending changes in lifestyle. In the medical profession, our thinking has traditionally been that healthy people generally are happier people. We could express this view in a simple diagram:

Health ⟶ Greater Happiness

Today, the findings of psychoneuroimmunology are coaxing us to a complementary view—that happier people can be healthier people. In other words:

Happiness ⟶ Greater Health

Or, to be more accurate:

Greater Happiness ⟷ Greater Health

When it comes to health and happiness, then, the arrows representing cause and effect go in both directions. Are we happy because we are healthy or healthy because we are happy? The answer to both questions is—yes!

It's here that knowledge of acting technique can play such a powerful role. After all, it's an actor's job to experience and portray the whole spectrum of human emotion. Could actors give us some tips on how to access the feelings that promote health—emotions we label happiness, serenity, optimism, and even love? This is where a man named Stanislavski enters the stage.

Stanislavski— patron saint of medicine

Constantin Stanislavski was one of the giants of twentieth-century theater. This Russian actor, director, and teacher of actors developed a system of acting so well known today that it is often called simply the "Method."

As you'll discover later in this book, one of Stanislavski's aims was to help actors evoke emotions—especially the emotions they needed to play their roles on stage with conviction. I believe that the Method is a gold mine of wisdom not only for those who live the life of the stage but those who live on the stage of life—that is, you and me.

In his efforts to create a powerful method of acting and a living form of theater art, Stanislavski uncovered many basic principles of physical and mental health. What's more, he expressed these principles in a practical way that invites us to action—to act well, and to act now.

Stanislavski anticipated many of the ideas now labeled alternative medicine. Already in the 1930s, Stanislavski taught that the mind and body are one (mind-body), and that changing the motions of the body and the thoughts of the mind would change the chemistry of feelings. In fact, this idea was at the core of the Method, making Stanislavski not only an astute actor, but an astute psychologist and applied physiologist as well.

The terms and techniques taught by Stanislavski give us a fresh, new way to talk about the basic insights of psychoneuroimmunology. One way to master this field is to invest weeks, months, or even years of careful study, combing through dry, scholarly journals. This book holds out another option: Take the short course instead. Through the forceful words of Stanislavski and the compelling metaphor of acting, take advantage of many of the most effective ideas that psychoneuroimmunology has uncovered. Learn how acting can help access feelings that promote your health and alter the very chemistry of your body.

Stanislavski's strategies for effective acting fall under three broad categories:

- Physical—changes in movement, speech, gesture, and costume. Included in this category is verbal as well as nonverbal behavior. And don't forget basic health practices such as hygiene, nutrition, breathing, and exercise. All of them are key to preparing for the person you want to be—in theater terms, the character role you want to play.

- Mental—changes in thinking, beliefs, images, and self-dialogue. The whole subject of mental preparation connects closely to what playwrights do when they create a powerful script.

- Staging—All the details used to "set the stage" fall in this category. This is where you pay attention to scenery, props, lighting, sounds, and smells, as well as your supporting cast—the people with whom you'd like to share the "stage" of your daily life.

We can sum up these ideas with the following diagram:

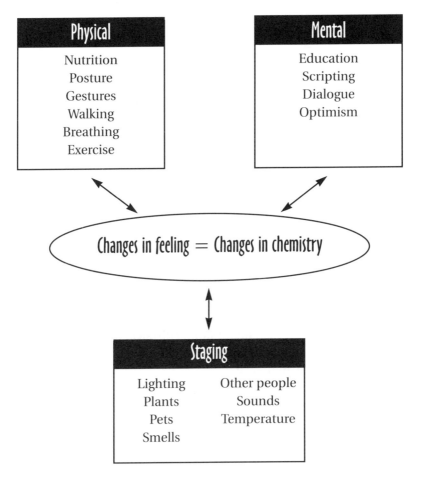

Physical

Nutrition
Posture
Gestures
Walking
Breathing
Exercise

Mental

Education
Scripting
Dialogue
Optimism

Changes in feeling = Changes in chemistry

Staging

Lighting   Other people
Plants   Sounds
Pets   Temperature
Smells

In essence, *Act Now* explains how the ideas captured in this diagram could make a difference in your experience of health. The steps to health, happiness, and even wealth often follow the same scripting and the same staging. When we act well, we create a more satisfying role on the stage of daily life.

ACT NOW!

Physicians get into the act

Is it so strange to suggest that physicians and other professionals draw on the wisdom of actors and the techniques of the stage?

"Medicine and the theatre have long been linked," wrote Chris McManus in a 1994 issue of *Lancet*, the prestigious British medical journal. "Shakespeare seemingly had a wide knowledge of medicine, Moliere and George Bernard Shaw wrote plays about doctors, Chekov and Somerset Maugham were doctors who wrote plays, Dr. Jonathan Miller directs plays, and most medical schools have their amateur dramatics."

In the same issue, physicians Hillel M. Finestone and David B. Conter take this idea even further. "We think that doctors must be actors—better actors than they are now," note Finestone and Conter. In fact, they call on medical schools to include courses in acting as part of the standard curriculum. Defending this idea, Finestone and Conter write:

> There is already a clear and constant acting component in the practice of medicine, although physicians are not always aware of this and are rarely trained to use it purposefully and many may try to deny it. . . .
>
> I find it essential to convey an encouraging, hopeful, often cajoling message to the patient to communicate concern. . . . These messages are important because they address the emotional needs of the patient and those around him, and I believe they have a clear impact on the patient's quality of life and extent and speed of recovery. However, I am not in the same frame of mind every day. I may be tired, angry, or concerned about an unwell family member. On such occasions, *I must, in effect, act to convey the responsiveness and concern that I believe have an important effect on the patient's health.*

I can hear some of you objecting, charging that physicians who act this way are dishonest and even manipulative. Many would prefer that their physicians be "real," refrain from acting, and show genuine empathy and feeling for their patients.

Finestone and Conter are sensitive to this objection. Yet, as they point out, empathy is hard to define and even harder to practice on a full-time basis. The basic problem is that we cannot directly command our emotions.

Given the pace of a physician's day and the demands of the job, there will come times when physicians feel little or no empathy—no matter how hard they try. Sometimes being "real" isn't good enough.

In this case, physicians have an alternative. They can act concerned and compassionate. That is, they can gesture and speak as if they feel empathy. Besides comforting the patient, this strategy may even trigger the desired, positive feelings in the physician as well.

From doctor to "witch doctor"

In his book *Space, Time and Medicine*, physician Larry Dossey narrates a vivid example of the physician as actor. A man named Jim entered the hospital with an admitting diagnosis of cancer. He had lost 50 pounds in six months. Emaciated and weak, Jim wore what Dossey calls the "look of death." This was tragic enough. Yet even more distressing to Jim's physicians was another fact: Two weeks of the usual diagnostic tests showed no sign of cancer. All results were normal. Jim was dying, and his physicians had no idea why.

Eventually Jim confessed that he knew the reason for his condition. "Doctor," he said, "I've been hexed." According to Jim, an enemy

ACT NOW!

had hired a shaman to steal a lock of Jim's hair and put a curse on it. According to the shaman, this meant Jim was doomed to die, and Jim believed so, too. The day he found out about the hex, Jim stopped eating. He'd come to the hospital to die.

Jim's physician, aware that every conventional medical treatment had failed, tried the only option he could think of: a midnight ceremony to "de-hex" Jim. During this ceremony, the physician cut another lock of Jim's hair and burned it. While this took place, the physician said, "As the fire burns your hair, the hex in your body is destroyed. But if you reveal this ceremony to anyone, the hex will return immediately, stronger than before!"

Jim took part in the ceremony with a combination of terror and respect. More importantly, he fully accepted the power of the de-hexing ceremony. He awoke the next morning and ordered a triple serving of breakfast and double servings of each following meal. After several days, Jim left the hospital as a well man, leaving behind a stack of normal test results.

This incident reminds us of something that's easy to forget. Medicine and the theater share common historical roots. Both emerged from religious ritual, and I can easily imagine that some of those early rituals involved shamanistic practices.

For all their differences, actors and shamans enter common ground on at least one point. Under certain conditions, both can trigger altered states of consciousness in themselves and in others. Both can transform their everyday self and taking on the chemistry of another personality.

For the shaman, this "other" is often the spirit of an animal, god, or dead person. For the actor, the "other" is the spirit of a fictional character created by the playwright. In a real sense, both shamans and actors perform in unseen realms, conjuring up formerly unseen realities. Indeed, religion, healing, and drama probably have grown from the same art roots: the art of caring for others.

Mrs. Becker visits the "touch doctor"

I first heard about acting as a healing technique when I was a 10-year-old lad in Austin, a small town in rural southern Minnesota. I didn't realize it then, but a meaningful part of my medical education began in this friendly environment, the roots of my rich Scandinavian heritage.

I remember hearing certain phrases over and over again when I was a boy: *It's all in the head.* Imagine that. Isn't that touching? At the time I didn't understand that these homely slogans contained profound medical wisdom.

The first time I remember hearing "It's all in the head" was in the heated discussion that surrounded Mrs. Becker's "miracle" cure. Mrs. Becker lived two houses down the road from us. She had been on crutches for as long as I could remember. During all those years she complained of pain in her hips and back. Her frenzied search for help had taken her from physician to physician, but each treatment—whether from physicians, chiropractors or physical therapists—failed to restore her health.

At last she was convinced by a kindly neighbor to "experience the magic of the laying on of hands." So Mrs. Becker decided to see the "touch doctor" who made a weekly visit to Rose Creek, a town about 10 miles away. One Thursday afternoon, after a visit to the touch doctor, Mrs. Becker returned without her crutches. She had left them in Rose Creek. I never saw her on crutches again.

ACT NOW!

I was 10 years old when this happened, a time I mark as the beginning of my medical education. And I can still hear my Aunt Vera talking about Mrs. Becker. Every family must have an Aunt Vera. My own is someone whose wonderful laugh resounds in my mind even though she's been gone many years.

Aunt Vera would roll her eyes, shake her head a bit, and laugh. "Ha, ha, ha, ha. Mrs. Becker—she went off to see the touch doctor. Isn't that touching? Left her crutches there in Rose Creek. Obviously whatever she had all these years was all in the head. Imagine that."

"It's all an act," another neighbor would chime in. "Either she was acting before she went to Rose Creek or she is putting on an act now."

About the same time, one of my cousins graduated from college and went to Europe. He brought back photographs of all the places he'd visited. The ones I remember most vividly were pictures of Lourdes, a Roman Catholic shrine in southwest France. These pictures showed much cast-off paraphernalia of ill health—thousands of crutches, braces, canes, and wheelchairs. To an impressionable lad of 10, this was truly remarkable.

In 1858, legend has it, the Virgin Mary appeared at Lourdes to a 14-year-old peasant girl, now known as St. Bernadette. Each year three million people visit Lourdes, many of them on crutches, wearing braces, or using wheelchairs and hoping for a miracle like the one that happened to St. Bernadette. Many of these people report cures after their visit to the holy site.

You can guess the prevailing opinion of my family and neighbors about those pictures. They simply echoed Aunt Vera: "Those people who get cured that way—well, whatever they had was (ha, ha) all in the head. Imagine that. They just changed their act!"

Placebos as an act

Years later, when I was in medical school, I took part in testing new experimental pain medications. It was standard procedure in these studies to give one group of patients a placebo, a simple sugar pill that had no medicinal properties whatever. These patients, however, thought they were getting a powerful new pain medication. Another group of patients took a "real" new pain medication. Later we compared results from people taking the actual medication with the results from those who'd taken the placebo.

To our surprise, the sugar pill effectively relieved pain about 40 percent of the time. By contrast, the actual pain medication was about 90 percent effective. Keeping with standard research practice, we threw out the results from the placebo. The placebo effect was a contaminant, we thought, caused by "tricks of the mind." Our reaction was merely a sophisticated version of Aunt Vera's. "Obviously, anyone who experienced pain relief with a sugar pill had a pain that was all in the head," she would have said. "Imagine that."

After my training in general surgery at the Mayo Clinic, my wife and I went to Ethiopia as members of the Peace Corps. To say that we were stretched thin is an understatement. There were 20 million people in Ethiopia, and I was one of 19 physicians there at the time.

We would go on medical safaris to many of the remote villages to give small pox vaccinations and other immunizations to the children. Villagers would often ask us to see and care for some of their leaders. Often we had little more than aspirin, vitamin tablets, and malaria pills.

At one of these villages a group appeared with their chief, who was complaining of weakness and pains. These people demanded (in a rather threatening way) more than just a pill for the chief: "Doesn't the American doctor have a shot?" They were becoming quite insis-

ACT NOW!

tent. Indeed, I was concerned and somewhat frightened by their demands.

Fortunately that day in my doctor's "bag of tricks" I did have a syringe with a relatively large needle and a vial of 50 percent glucose (sugar) water. I simply drew two cubic centimeters of the sugar water into my syringe and administered a shot in the buttocks of the chief. Sugar water has a special sting, so he felt the "power" of the medicine (and in all likelihood had a painful rear end for several weeks).

When I returned to that same village several months later, I was greeted with a joyful reception: "Where's the great American doctor?" The leader embraced me, exclaiming that he'd received the magic medicine from the magic needle and now felt so much better! Of course, I knew, along with my wife and the other Peace Corps volunteers, that it was "all in the head." Unfortunately, Vera wasn't there to add, "Ha, ha, ha—imagine that."

The next step in my career was a position with the Indian Health Service in Gallup, New Mexico. I was a surgeon working with the Hopi, the Navajo, and the Zuni Indians. The night before a Navajo underwent surgery, it was common to find their medicine men in our ward, dressed in beads, feathers, and full healing regalia.

These practitioners of the Navajo healing ceremony danced around the bed of the Navaho patients, singing sacred chants. The ceremonial "stage" was replete with ritualistic costumes, props, incense, and rhythms. And frequently the Navaho patients who took part in these rituals recovered more quickly and with fewer complications than patients who did not get visits from the dancing healers.

Decades later I found myself working in the biomechanics clinic of the orthopedic department at one of the largest medical clinics in America, Park Nicollet Medical Center in Minneapolis. I saw many people with chronic aches and pains. Some of them were referred to me after living with a pain in their back or joints for months. They'd call my receptionist and say, "I can't take it any more. I have to get in to Dr. Anderson and see what this pain is all about. Someone must fix me!"

Sometimes my receptionist would respond, "I'm very sorry but the earliest I can get you in is three weeks from today." I regretted such delays, and so did the people who called me. But they usually waited, and finally I did get to see them.

When the date of the office visit finally arrived, I greeted these people and asked them to tell me about the pain they'd been living with. At this point the patient often appeared a little nervous, perhaps a little bewildered.

"I hate to say it, but that pain I called about—you know, the one I've had for months? Well, I'm finally here to see you and . . . well . . . this has been a pretty good day. I can't explain it, but amazingly enough, I feel much better. You know Doc, people always feel better the day they go see the doctor. Maybe it's all in the head." (Imagine that!)

As I listened to these words, I was standing in an impressive clinic in my official-looking white coat, the official costume of the modern healer. I was seeing people who'd been scheduled by my official-sounding receptionist. And close to my office was a medical laboratory and rooms full of high-tech equipment—part of the staging, props, and scenery of a modern medical clinic. All this, and even though I hadn't touched the patient in front of me, she was already better.

I am perplexed by all this—perhaps even a little scared, because the touch doctor who came through Rose Creek when I was 10 years old was eventually run out of town by the medical and government authorities. And now, more than 50 years after that healing miracle in Rose Creek, I wonder: Doesn't every physician have some power

ACT NOW!

•••

to dispense "healing chemistry"—a power in some ways analogous to that dispensed by shamans and other unconventional healers?

Did Mrs. Becker have an illness that was in the head or did she have a cure that was "in the head"? And did the change in Mrs. Becker induce a healthy new act? In this book, I argue that in all probability, it did. So why aren't we getting *everybody* into the act.

Confronted with such questions, I again asked, Why? Why do people experience relief from shots of sugar water or rituals of shamans? Why do they feel better after merely making a medical appointment or entering a physician's office?

Today I believe that the study of the theater points us toward some answers. And those answers have to do with costuming, staging, scripting, gestures, tone of voice—topics that actors deal with during every performance. Perhaps healthcare providers and patients also need to more fully understand how to act.

Life is theater

Shakespeare wrote, "All the world's a stage, and all the men [and women] merely players. They have their exits and entrances, and one in time plays many parts." This playwright knew we all occupy many stages in the course of our lives, even in the course of a single day.

Actually this saying, like all such sayings, oversimplifies things. Of course, life is different than theater. The point of this book is that the dynamics of life and theater overlap, and that comparing daily life to the role of an actor on stage offers some illuminating insights. Words that point to the power of acting in changing human behavior are even part of our everyday parlance. For example, we speak of role models and role playing. We know people who

•••

act old or act young, who act tough or act stupid. I even know some who act sick and others who act happy and healthy. It's the act of happiness and health that this book will prescribe.

Shakespeare could have gone on to say, Oh, we all have many different roles. We wear many different costumes, many postures, many facial configurations and hair styles. But we also create thousands of images in our minds. We read and write many different lines for ourselves—scripts of happiness, sadness, success, and failure. What's more, we set the various stages of our lives in hundreds of ways, and each one of these sets affects our mind-body chemistry as we play our various roles in life.

Whenever I speak about these ideas, I feel compelled to convince people that it's okay to act. It's fine to take on a role that doesn't feel right at the present moment. It's fine to realize you are "sincerely insincere" when you are are playing the role of a happy, healthy person who hasn't quite got the hang of it yet.

Even actors may need convincing on this point. After a particularly upbeat performance, actors will often say they were really "on," or the "chemistry was on" between audience and actors.

The question I've often addressed to performing artists is this: If you felt that good, healthy chemistry while acting on stage, why not act off stage? If acting feels so good on stage, why not use the same techniques to promote your health and happiness in daily life?

The answer I often get is, "Well, it's just not real to act when you're offstage." This answer testifies to an image problem that actors have had for centuries. In fact, the ancient Greek word for actor, *hypokritos*, implied two-facedness and deceit. As George Burns said, "The trick to being a good actor is to be sincere. And once you can fake sincerity, you've got it made!"

But, I reply to the actors, you acted real on stage. Your part must have felt real enough at the moment of performance. After all, how do actors transform themselves into their characters for the duration of a play? They do so by using certain techniques and cultivating certain habits that eventually become second nature.

If the notion of acting your way to better health presents difficulties for you, then I suggest a small change in terminology. Instead of acting, think of yourself as performing a more powerful part. Perhaps the notion of a great performance review or of making your life a great performance will be more to your liking.

Think of creating a new "real." I know the real me isn't good enough. I want to develop a new, healthier "real" me. To do so I will need to act on making some new habits—act on making some new chemistry. And when that new, healthy chemistry begins to feel normal, I will be a new "real." And then I can start working on another even newer, better "real."

You can change

One of my assumptions is that human beings are malleable. People can change. In response, you may be thinking, "So, you're saying that I can become anybody I want to be, that I have no inherent personality. That must mean I'm a blank slate, just clay willing to be shaped, ready to be anything I want."

Actually, I'm not making such a sweeping statement. Obviously we have limits. All of us must live with our genetic makeup—the physical "costume" we've been issued. At my age, for example, I am never going to get a basketball scholarship to the University of Minnesota. And at 5 feet, 7 inches and 130 pounds, I'm never going to be a sumo wrestler.

What I am saying is this: Within the limits imposed by chance and heredity, you have a big element of choice, perhaps more than you realize.

Each of us makes moment-by-moment choices about what to say, how to gesture, how to stand, how to breathe, and much more. The point of *Act Now* is that such choices can have a profound effect on our health. What's more, the techniques of acting can help us make these choices with more clarity and power—and fun.

For David Reynolds, the whole experience of changing from professor to mental patient to professor again threw into question the very notion of a stable identity. Is any one of us really just one, static personality? After his experiences as a mental patient, Reynolds answered:

> There is a sense in which the experiential researcher really becomes another person. Inconceivable? Trivial? Merely a word game? Perhaps not. For a long time we in the social sciences have operated on the assumption that a normal human being is or has a single enduring identity or personality. . . . But now, on the basis of my research experience, I have also been David Kent and David Randolph . . . both of whom felt and behaved in ways that Reynolds never has.

To me, this is a great statement of human potential. We've heard Shakespeare's old saw so often that we gloss over its true power. He understood that our lives are a succession of roles played out on various stages. Yet, as actors know, none of us has to play just one role for life. If we don't like the character we're playing, we can choose a new role, create a new character with a new chemistry, and walk onto a new stage.

Think about that for a minute. Suppose that the person you are today is not the person you want to be. Say that there are days when you long to remake yourself and become someone different. Do you have to be content with the person you are today and settle for living life at a fraction of your potential?

My answer is No. You can change yourself to a degree that will probably surprise you. This is especially true when it comes to matters of health. Just as David Reynolds acted himself sick, you can explore the possibility of acting yourself well. And the chemistry of a happy act is probably the chemistry that makes for better health.

I offer these ideas not as a panacea or a prescription. No one can guarantee that using acting techniques will transform your health. As a physician, I always emphasize that these techniques are not a cure-all. I am not saying that people who change their thinking and actions can necessarily rid themselves of all aches and pains. Nor am I saying that they can be free of arthritis, infections, or cancers.

However, there is one thing I *do* want to suggest: Acting can help you think in new ways, feel better, and behave more effectively. And all this change can make your life more enjoyable. Though it is not intended to replace conventional western medicine, the chemistry that you create through acting "well" may enhance the modern health care that we are fortunate enough to experience.

The principles in *Act Now* can become an adjunctive therapy that both you and your physician can use. And although the ideas in this book are not guaranteed to add days to your life, they can add life to your days.

SCENE ONE

....

START WITH CHEMISTRY

Think of the references we hear in daily life to the power of chemistry:

> *"When I get together with her, we just seem to click.*
> *The chemistry is just right."*

> *"The chemistry between people in this office is great."*

> *"When I hire someone, I'm looking for a person who's*
> *got the right chemistry for the job."*

We often talk about the chemistry of a good relationship, the chemistry of a place, the chemistry of a task. We also say that chemistry is contagious.

If you smile at me, I'll usually smile back at you. If you start laughing, chances are that I will, too. Why do we often smile at people and say a few pleasant words when we meet them for the first time? Because this simple act, this humble performance, changes the chemistry of a relationship in a way we both value.

It also works in the opposite way. The wall plaque I recently saw hanging in a kitchen says it all: "When Momma ain't happy, there ain't nobody happy!" David Sobel, coauthor of a wonderful book titled *Healthy Pleasures*, offers a similar example. On one occasion when he was "wound up tight," his young son said, "Daddy, when you act like that, I feel bad!" At that moment, the boy experienced some of the Dr. Sobel's unhealthy chemistry.

Most of us can testify that it's hard to feel "up" around people who feel angry, depressed, or lethargic. We can almost sense the vital energy draining out of our bodies.

All these comments about chemistry point to a useful truth. When we say that the chemistry of a relationship is good, we're saying something that can literally be true.

Feelings are chemistry

Substitute the word feeling for the word chemistry. When your feelings change, your biochemistry changes also. Look at a person whose shoulders are hunched, whose breathing is shallow, with eyes cast downward, and a face that's frozen into a frown. This person's body chemistry will differ from the person who's smiling, breathing deeply, making eye contact, and leaning toward you for a hug. Those differences in chemistry may be extensive or subtle, but they're always significant.

Feelings and chemistry, then, are intertwined. They are one and the same. And as a physician, I'm compelled to ask the next logical questions: How do feelings and health connect? By cultivating states of positive feeling, can we change our chemistry and improve our health? Will people who consistently experience loving relationships, satisfying work, and optimism about the future be healthier than those who consistently feel unloved, unsatisfied, and pessimistic?

These are some questions driving a relatively new field in medical research—psychoneuroimmunology. This is a new field with a long name. Yet behind all the fancy terminology is a simple assertion: The mind and body are one. Feelings are physiological and chemical realities that permeate every aspect of the mind-body. The chemistry of our thoughts and actions resonate throughout the mind-body. What we think, how we act, and what we feel dramatically affects our immunity—our ability to stay well.

By the way, please don't be put off by that long name. To understand the word psychoneuroimmunology, just split it into three parts:

• Psycho

> refers to mental processes—thoughts, beliefs, mental images, and feelings.

• Neuro

> relates to the chemistry of the nervous system (the brain and spinal cord), as well as hormones that regulate human emotion.

• Immunology

> refers to the body's ability to resist disease and various kinds of infection.

In that long word is a more complete image of the human being than we've ever had in medicine before. Mind, body, immunity—all are there, present, and accounted for. And the fact that all three concepts are part of the same word implies that they're related. In any one place in the body—in each and every single cell—these three factors are intermeshed. Our body is our mind-immunity, our mind is our body-immunity, and our immunity is our body-mind.

Mind and body separated

When my generation of physicians was in medical school, we didn't always make this connection. We were taught to look for "RD"—real disease. As a result, we saw most diseases as physical disorders. Sure, there was a small group of conditions labeled "psychosomatic" that were affected by a patient's emotions and mental outlook. But we saw these conditions as outside the mainstream of our medical practice and often relegated them to psychiatrists and psychologists.

Meanwhile, the rest of us focused our attention on "real" illnesses with "real" physical causes. During my early years of clinical practice, my interest and that of many of my colleagues was in the body—not the mind. If I couldn't treat a patient with a pill or fix their problem with surgery, then they needed a psychiatrist—or worse yet, no one could help them.

In separating the mind from the body and sending patients off to different specialists, we paid our debt to a stream of thinking at least 400 years old. A leading voice in that tradition was Rene Descartes, a French philosopher and the man who's often quoted as saying, "I think, therefore I am."

Descartes' aim was to find a reliable foundation for knowledge of the world. Much of his writing focused on dualism—the idea that mind and body are strictly separate and operate independently of each other. This idea circulated throughout the learned people of Europe, paving ground for the modern scientific method. (Ironically, the concept of the scientific method came to Descartes in a dream.)

We can almost imagine a meeting between Descartes and the Pope sometime in the seventeenth century. After some haggling, the mighty philosopher could have struck a bargain.

"Okay, I leave matters of the mind and spirit to you," he'd have said to the Pope. "You get to deal with emotions, beliefs, intuition, and all that other murky stuff that's so hard to observe. But you leave science and knowledge of the physical world to me. I want to deal with things and events that we can see, hear, feel, and measure in a precise way."

Although the meeting never happened, Western religion and science proceeded for the next several centuries as if it had. Western medicine pursued a secular track and clerics controlled the spiritual realm.

Mind and body reunited

This agreement to separate the mind from the body transformed the world. It gave birth to a science powerful enough to create radio, television, cars, computers, atom splitters, and fax machines.

In medicine, the scientific method allowed us to banish infectious diseases such as tuberculosis and smallpox in many parts of the world—conditions that once wiped out whole populations. The scientific method also created an army of pharmaceutical drugs and surgical procedures that saved even more lives. Indeed, science and mainstream medical practice have given us much to be thankful for.

Even so, this outlook on the world has limitations. It leaves a lot unaccounted for, such as the placebo effect (described later in this scene) and spontaneous remission from disease. The latter occurs when cancerous tumors shrink or other symptoms of disease disappear—all in the absence of administered drugs, surgery, or other standard treatments.

Most physicians learn about spontaneous remission, and many have patients who have experienced it. Until recently, this phenomenon has left us scratching our heads. Today, we are searching for clues to this mystery in the connection between the mind and the body. We're seriously considering the role of a patient's beliefs, emotions, and thoughts in the treatment of "real disease." Even the term psychosomatic illness has fallen out of favor, and we're acknowledging that most diseases have a mental component.

In short, we are just beginning to throw off the cloak of Descartes' logic. No longer can we separate mind and body and make sense of the world. There is startling evidence that every cell in our body has a "mind," that each element of the human being communicates with every other element. We are a chemical-thinking-physical-spiritual oneness. And leading the way in this line of thinking is the field of psychoneuroimmunology.

Cousins' "laughing cure" launches a movement

Psychoneuroimmunology gained public attention when a small book titled *Anatomy of an Illness,* by Norman Cousins, hit the best-seller lists. This was one of the first popular books to explore the connection between mind-body, between feeling and healing.

Cousins, editor of the *Saturday Review,* developed a painful and progressive condition called ankylosing spondylitis. This condition is often fatal. During a hospital stay, in fact, Cousins overheard one his physicians say, "I think we're losing Norman."

Shortly after that, Cousins, with the help of his doctors, took a more active role in his medical treatment. He checked out of the hospital and into a hotel, substituting a clinical atmosphere for one that was more like home. Cousins also paid rigorous attention to his mental and emotional state, reshaping his environment to stimulate happiness and laughter. He even arranged for private screenings of films by Laurel and Hardy and other classic comedians.

Soon the results became apparent. After beginning his self-prescribed regimen, Cousins' sedimentation rate (a measure of his body's inflammation) decreased significantly. (Talk about a link between feeling and chemistry!) What's more, he experienced a direct connection between positive emotions and pain relief.

"I made the joyous discovery," he recalled, "that 10 minutes of genuine belly laughter had an anesthetic effect and would give me at least two hours of pain-free sleep." Eventually Cousins ceased his formal medical treatment, completely cured of ankylosing spondylitis.

Besides writing a great deal about his illness and recovery, Cousins changed careers. He left the magazine business and joined the staff at UCLA Medical School. There he continued to investigate psychoneuroimmunology, working with physicians and respected researchers. From this early start, a great deal followed, including work with the giants in psychoneuroimmunology as documented in his book *Head First: The Biology of Hope*.

Along with the breakthroughs came misunderstanding and simplistic thinking. Some articles in the popular press, for example, reported that Cousins laughed himself back to health. Even Cousins never made that claim. Instead, he argued that laughter and other positive feelings played some role in his recovery and called for more research in this area.

Discovering the chemistry of healing

Today many are heeding that call, and their work is finding broad acceptance. You may have read some recent books about the connection between the mind and body, such as *Ageless Body, Timeless Mind* by Deepak Chopra or *The Healer Within* by Steven Locke and Douglas Colligan.

Perhaps you watched the enormously popular television series on this subject, Bill Moyers' "Healing and the Mind," or read the book of the same title. Behind all this work is a tantalizing idea—that mind and body are one, and that understanding their connection is crucial to our health.

Of course, we're still a long way from understanding the connection between thinking and healing, between feelings and immunity. But what we do know is reshaping the health care field.

For example, physicians who once relied on the curative powers of drugs or surgery are now referring patients to yoga teachers. A cardiologist named Dean Ornish recently demonstrated that people can actually *reverse* the effects of heart disease through lifestyle changes alone, including diet, exercise, and stress management. (These results are documented in a book, *Dr. Dean Ornish's Program for Reversing Heart Disease.*)

People with chronic, intractable pain are learning meditation through mainstream medical institutions, such as the Stress Reduction Clinic at the University of Massachusetts Medical Center at Worcester. (For details on this program, see the book *Full Catastrophe Living: Using the Wisdom of Your Body and Mind to Face Stress, Pain and Illness* by Jon Kabat-Zinn.)

A group of hospitals has affiliated with a nonprofit organization called Planetree to help develop a more healing hospital environment—a physical environment and system of delivery that are more user friendly, thus promoting the chemistry of health-happiness.

Closer to home, I'm honored to play a part in creating a new department of complementary medicine at Park Nicollet Clinic in Minneapolis. Through this department, we'll mount a search for what's valuable among all the treatments now labeled "alternative" or "holistic." In this effort, we're following the lead of the National Institutes of Health, which recently established an Office of Alternative Medicine.

These are just a few examples of how the medical community is responding to a vast search by the American public for validated, safe, cost-effective, complementary modes of healing.

A 1992 survey published in the *New England Journal of Medicine* gave one striking piece of evidence: One out of three Americans visited an "alternative" health practitioner during the previous twelve months. At the heart of this search is a question about the connection between mind and body, feeling and healing.

The tiger in the trees

The idea that emotional states are linked with chemical states is not new. We've known for years, for instance, about the fight-or-flight response in which the human body is flooded with adrenaline in the face of sudden anger or stress. This response was a lifesaver for our early ancestors when they were stalked by a tiger or woolly mammoth.

Today, we're more likely to feel fight-or-flight when we're stuck in traffic or about to get reprimanded. In these situations we're usually

....

not free to fight or flee. Instead, we merely experience the wear and tear on the mind and body commonly known as stress.

Adrenaline is just one of the chemicals linked to human feeling. There are many other chemicals (such as neuropeptides and gamma globulins) and cells (such as macrophages, T–cells, and N–cells) that help the body fight off infection. One member of this group has received a lot of press. I speak of the "inner uppers" that deliver a potent and natural high on life—the endorphins.

Endorphins and "emotional empowerment"

Actually, the endorphins are one small group of a larger chemical family known as the neuropeptides. This family boasts 50 to 60 members. However, it's those colorful cousins, the endorphins, that usually get the attention. (Note: To keep things simple, from here on, I'm going to join the popular press and use the word endorphins to refer to all the chemicals linked with psychoneuroimmunology.)

Some endorphins are produced by nerve cells and other body tissues. They have a chemical structure almost identical to synthetic or plant-derived injectable morphine. That means endorphins can deliver the kind of pain relief and euphoria associated with morphine.

What would you see if you could look inside a brain at work? The answer to this question is complex, but in essence you'd see a lot of fireworks—millions of tiny explosions. Neurons, or nerve cells, are the building blocks of the brain and spinal cord. These cells fire off electrical charges, communicating via chemicals to other nerve cells and muscles.

....

In essence, these charges and chemicals make up the messages the nervous system sends to the rest of the body, and those messages regulate our thoughts and moods. As brain researcher Robert Ornstein puts it, such chemicals are "words" the brain uses to communicate. The endorphins are one group of these nerve chemicals. And the "words" of the endorphins create a language that results in a script of health and happiness.

It started with a flower

Ironically enough, we first found out about endorphins by studying a flower—the poppy. Humans have used poppy juice, also known as opium, for thousands of years to reduce pain and stimulate pleasure. Morphine is the main active ingredient in opium, and it's still used to treat severe pain.

In the early 1970s, however, some scientists wondered why this substance from a plant had such a powerful effect on human beings. The answer, they guessed, is that the brain produces its own form of opiates—its own internal morphine.

What followed was a worldwide race, of sorts, to find these natural opiates. Two researchers from the University of Aberdeen in Scotland were the first to do so, in 1975. Since then, other internally produced opiates have been discovered in the human body, and there may be many more.

Back to the endorphins. These internally produced chemicals attach to cells at the same sites as injectable morphine and therefore affect us much as injectable morphine does. Endorphins can prevent certain other brain cells from transmitting impulses, giving endorphins the power to block pain and produce feelings of euphoria.

These effects make endorphins crucial ingredients in our "pharmacy within." That internal pharmacy has several advantages over the drugs you buy from a drugstore. For one, endorphins are free. The adverse side effects of endorphins are minimal or nonexistent. What's more, endorphins made inside the body are anywhere from 200 to 2,000 times more potent than injectable morphine.

One of the reasons many people become addicted to morphine-type substances is that they create a euphoria, a feeling of mental well-being. However, the more they use injectable morphine, the more their bodies turn down production of natural morphine (endorphins). After the addict stops using morphine or one of the morphine derivatives, it takes a long time for the body to recover its ideal endorphin-producing capabilities.

Raising endorphins is just an act

It is these gifts from our internal pharmacy—the endorphins—that create a feeling of elation, a euphoria that gets us high on life.

Though we don't understand exactly how they work, we have strong evidence that endorphins and related neuropeptides are raised by a wide range of activities. Among them are laughter, sex, exercise, positive mental images, satisfying relationships, setting and reaching goals, parties, meaningful rituals, and—yes—just believing that something will do us good. (I refer to the latter belief as the "Pollyanna approach to life" or "reverse paranoia.") All these practices get us into the act of healing.

The endorphins are lowered in certain people, such as those who have poor posture and those who are in poor physical condition or are deficient in what I call the "three S's"—stamina, strength, and stretching. People with chronic pain or stress may start to use up some of their endorphin stores, and those who depend regularly on pain-relieving medications may turn off their endorphin production.

Besides pleasant feelings and even euphoria, the benefits associated with raising the endorphins include pain relief, tension relief, and a strengthened immune system. Once the endorphins are raised, the muscles become more relaxed and tensions are eased.

Maybe you've had the experience of carrying a piece of heavy furniture with a friend when one of you said something funny. You probably had to put the object down because the muscles got so weak. This weakness was probably the relaxation response triggered by your laughter, which stimulated endorphin production.

Endorphins can also be raised merely by imagining that a medication or a treatment works. This technique can sometimes be used to relieve muscular tension, headaches, and back pain. Imagine tension flowing right out of your body, and let the endorphins do the rest. This is an example of pos"I"tive thinking—using positive thoughts to promote health.

Not only can physical pain be reduced by raising endorphins, but often a reduction in emotional pain comes as well. When the endorphins rise, the euphoric state that occurs helps to diminish depression, anger, or fear. This change in serum chemistry has great potential for clearing the mind and making mental space for positive emotions.

When the endorphins are elevated, the immune system also functions better. People who raise their endorphin levels usually have greater numbers of T-cells, N-cells, and gamma globulins. All of these internal substances effectively fight bacteria and viruses.

Many specialists who treat cancer, chronic disease, and AIDS patients believe that raising endorphin levels is an important factor in the survival rate of their patients. It appears that stimulating the endorphins and related chemicals even correlates with a longer and healthier life.

Many other benefits may accompany increased endorphins. People who know how to raise endorphin levels, not only in themselves but also in others, are often popular, physically attractive, and report more confidence, creativity, courage, and control over their lives than their endorphin-poor peers.

A lifestyle full of endorphin-raising activities may even be associated with higher incomes. (We can genuinely say raising endorphins makes cents.) Individuals who can raise and keep endorphin levels high have been shown to relate better to themselves, their families, friends, and people in general.

We can't say there's a direct cause-effect relationship between raised endorphins and all the social, physical, and emotional benefits just named. Raising your endorphin level won't guarantee you higher income, better relationships, creativity, and all the rest.

So far all we can say is that such benefits are *associated* with raised endorphin levels—not *caused* by those endorphin levels. Yet that association is strong enough to merit serious attention. I for one am convinced that the connection is obvious.

When you act in ways that raise the endorphins, you're filling a powerful prescription from your pharmacy within. Another means to this end lies in placebos.

The power of placebos

The word *placebo* comes from the Latin word meaning "I shall please." The placebo effect demonstrates that our hopes, expectations, faith, and confidence in the "healer" may often be as important as the medication or treatment we receive. The placebo effect is compounded if the healthcare provider is well liked and pleasing to the patient, because then the patient wants to get better to please the provider.

We know, for instance, that people sometimes get excellent treatment results by merely ingesting a simple sugar or starch pill that they believe is powerful. And the "pleasing" result is compounded if both the giver and the receiver believe that the sugar pill is effective. How and who gives the placebo and what they believe are often just as important as to whom it is being given.

In their book *Healthy Pleasures*, brain researcher Robert Ornstein and physician David Sobel review research on the placebo effect. Their conclusion: Placebos are potent medicines that have relieved headaches, coughs, toothaches, postoperative pain, angina, asthma, warts, and other conditions. "It appears," they write, "that no symptom or system is immune to the placebo effect."

Ornstein and Sobel cite one study of a woman suffering from severe nausea and vomiting. After trying several conventional treatments, which failed, her physicians said they were giving her a "new and extremely powerful wonder drug." This drug, they said, was certain to relieve her nausea. Twenty minutes after taking this drug, the woman's nausea disappeared.

What was the wonder drug? Syrup of ipecac, a medicine long used to induce vomiting. Here the placebo effect was powerful enough to reverse the normal effect of the medication.

ACT NOW!

....

It no longer surprises me when I read studies concluding that a 35 to 45 percent reduction of pain comes from the placebo effect alone. In fact, that figure may be too low. In his book *Health and Healing,* physician Andrew Weil argues convincingly that the placebo effect involves the beliefs of the health care provider as well as the beliefs of the patient.

This was substantiated by a 1994 article in the *Journal of the American Medical Association,* which reported that the percentage of patients responding to a sham or placebo treatment can be doubled from 35 to 70 percent if the health care provider believes in the drug or procedure. Several examples in the article involved surgical procedures judged to be effective largely because of the "magic wand " (the placebo effect) of the scalpel. Again, these procedures involved the beliefs of both patient and surgeon.

Unfortunately, there is no way to do "double blind" surgical studies that would scientifically quantitate the effects of the patient's and provider's beliefs. All the outcome studies of surgical procedures are enhanced by the positive belief system attributed to them by the surgeon and the patient.

I can only speculate that this two-part placebo effect involves an element of theater or even religious ritual. For example, present-day surgery bears an uncanny resemblance to ancient ritualistic surgery performed in healing shrines by the high priests of the Aztecs and Incas. In the following passage, I paraphrase remarks on this subject by Dr. Jerome Frank from a 1975 article in *The Johns Hopkins Medical Journal:*

> The operating room theater of today has provocative similarities to the ceremonies that occurred when the Aztec Priests performed trehpining procedures (drilling holes in the skull) to release evil spirits. The healing shrine's servants are organized into many

....

echelons, each having its own insignia of rank and function. The priesthood (surgeons and operating personnel) communicated in a special language, unintelligible to the layman, and prominently displayed on their person healing costumes (like modern surgical "scrubs", masks, and headdress) and healing amulets and charms (like modern scalpels). These priests were expected to dedicate themselves to the service of the shrine, regardless of personal hardships or interference with connubial felicity and other satisfactions. The inner "holy" chamber for the "ultimate" ritual of healthcare was accessible only through special doors. The priests and designated assistants could enter these doors only after donning special dress and undergoing purification rites. The mysteries of the inner chamber altar (operating room and table) were jealously guarded.

Today, placebos are no longer dismissed as quack remedies. Medical researchers are beginning to acknowledge their medicinal power, even though we don't understand how placebos work. It could be that they stimulate the brain, endocrine system, and adrenal glands to act in ways that heal the body.

Also, beliefs and placebos may alleviate pain by triggering the release of endorphins and related chemicals. Evidence for this possibility comes from a study of people who underwent dental surgery to extract wisdom teeth. They received an intravenous injection of what they were told was a "very powerful" pain medication. In reality, that medication was a placebo. Forty percent of these people reported significant relief of pain. In addition, blood analyses confirmed that those who experienced pain relief had an elevation in endorphins.

Next, the "placebo responding" group was given Nalaxone, a drug that blocks morphines and morphine-like chemicals such as endorphins. They immediately reported an increase in pain thus supporting the idea that endorphins were responsible for the pain relief.

"Whatever the precise pathways through mind and body," wrote Norman Cousins in *Anatomy of an Illness*, "enough evidence already exists to indicate that placebos can be as potent as—and sometimes more potent than—the active drugs they replace." Cousins even went on to say that the history of medicine may be the history of the placebo effect.

Choose a positive role

The placebo effect brings to mind another aspect of positive belief—one that's related to acting. It's been shown that the endorphins can be "faked" up. For instance, forcing a smile or a laugh can fool the endorphins into life. That's a great reason for laughing more, even if the situation isn't necessarily funny. Consciously being more optimistic and looking for the humorous side of everyday events can give us that inner high.

Be forewarned that if you talk about faking good feelings, you might be accused of being a Pollyanna, of seeing the world through rose-colored glasses, or being an incurable optimist. Even worse, a friend who has read lots of self-help books may say you're in denial.

My reply is that Pollyanna got a bad rap. Consider this: All of us live by illusions. None of us really sees the world as it is. Instead, we see the world as we are.

There's a physiological reason for this. One of the main jobs of the human brain is to filter out a vast array of sense impressions. Those perceptions are coming at us at the rate of hundreds per second. Suppose you could be conscious of every thought, sight, sound, smell, taste, and body sensation you experienced. Talk about being burned out—you'd be on sensory overload!

Sorting things out

Mercifully, our brains filter out most impressions so we can concentrate on what matters most. Think of the brain as a file clerk who can move faster than the speed of light. This clerk sorts our perceptions into piles marked "attend to this first," "act on this later," and "ignore." But what determines which sensory impressions go into the "attend to this first" pile? There are many factors, but our attitudes and general view, our script of the world plays a central role.

Take the student who has a passionate conviction that his career options are limited. What news stories is he more apt to notice? Chances are they'll be the latest unemployment figures, plant closings, and layoffs. In short, he takes in data that confirms his existing view of the world. This, in turn, discourages him from putting effort into career planning and job hunting.

Now take another student with roughly the same abilities and interests. Her general outlook is different, however. She believes her career options are virtually limitless, provided she plans carefully and cultivates her favorite skills. When she opens the morning paper, she's more likely to focus on stories that confirm her view, such as tips for successful interviewing and resumes and articles on interesting places to work.

Which person has "turned on" the chemistry of personal success? It's impossible to prove either person right or wrong, and perhaps both of their views are illusory to some degree. But it does seem

....

obvious that the optimistic person is more likely to experience career satisfaction.

I'd place my bets with the optimistic woman. Many professionals in career planning hold that successful job hunting is primarily a function of choice, commitment, and action. The person with the optimistic outlook is more likely to display these qualities. Perhaps she is living by an illusion, but her illusions serve her well.

Illusions and free will

Many of the crucial issues of life present us with such options. The philosopher William James once said that he could not conclusively prove whether human beings have free will. Yet he decided to *act as if* he had free will, because this view led to a more satisfying life. He, too, chose the illusion that served him best.

I go into this point in some detail because of the roles that optimism and favorable attitudes play in raising endorphins and creating good health. We're learning more about this all the time. For example, psychologist Suzanne Kobasa and her colleagues at the University of Chicago studied executives at AT&T when that company was undergoing corporate reorganization and layoffs. This was a time of great stress for most AT&T managers. Yet some executives remained generally healthy, while others succumbed to a variety of illnesses.

Kobasa concluded that the more healthy executives had a set of attitudes that focused on three qualities.

• First, they had a strong commitment to work and family.

• Second, they felt they were still in control of the overall quality of their lives. They lived by the saying, "If it is to be, it is up to me."

- And finally, they viewed change as a challenge rather than a threat.

In short, these people developed an optimistic script for themselves—and those optimistic attitudes registered in their bodies as well as their minds.

Feeling good is no cure-all

Before leaving this topic of positive attitudes and health, I want to make one more point. I'm excited by the ground swell of interest in visualization, laughter, affirmations, prayer, and positive emotions as aids in overcoming illness. At the same time, we cannot expect to smile automatically or laugh ourselves to perfect health. It's regrettably easy for people to inflict feelings of failure on themselves if they're unable to bring about miracle cures through these methods.

Self-blame can enter here. People who suffer certain illnesses such as cancer, arthritis, chronic pain, or repeated infections might blame themselves for harboring negative attitudes and failing to relate to people. They can get the idea that their illness is something they wished or secretly willed upon themselves through flawed lifestyles.

While lifestyle is a crucial component of health, we must emphasize that any illness has many facets and many causes. Rarely is one aspect of our lifestyle the sole cause of a disease. Obviously, factors such as sanitation, air and water quality, accidents, genetics, and many more can play a significant role outside of our individual control.

To say that the mind and emotions contribute significantly to physical health is not to say they are the only factors involved. Rather, many factors are at work in developing any state of health:

exercise, nutrition, alcohol abuse, caffeine abuse, smoking, shift work, poor sleep, negative attitudes, financial problems, accidents, genetics, and feeling out of control or not being connected to people. Any one of these many factors piled on top of other existing factors may be the proverbial "straw that breaks the camel's back" to cause disease.

At any rate, I find it most constructive to concentrate on what people can do in the present to improve their health, along with the meaning and quality of their lives. This approach is far more effective than speculating on the ways they might have created an illness.

Chemistry changes the "soil" of immunity

The topic of immunity raises a fascinating question. During an epidemic where hundreds of people are exposed to an infectious disease, why do some people get sick and others remain well? The question is much like the one gardeners ask: When you plant a flower bed, why do some seeds flourish and others flounder?

It both cases, the answer lies not only in the quality and quantity of the seeds but in the soil. Some soil is richer, more alive with vital nutrients that plants crave. Other soil is depleted and wasted, making it almost impossible for seeds to grow. You could toss a hundred seeds into the latter soil, all without much reward in the way of blooming flowers. The chemistry of the soil just isn't right.

In a similar way, we need the kind of chemistry that enriches the "soil" of the human immune system. When we understand the intimate link between mind and body, we can take a new approach to health—one that's based on changing our chemistry. We can bolster our immunity by using our minds in new ways. We can adopt beliefs that serve our health rather than undermine it. We can make conscious use of the placebo effect. And we can cultivate feelings that release the physician within—our internal pharmacy of healing chemicals.

I see this new scientific evidence for connection between mind and body, between emotions and health, as the most important medical development in my 36 years as a physician. I also believe that a knowledge of acting may be the most direct way to take advantage of these findings. Through the study of acting techniques, we can learn how to make the right moves and think the right thoughts that invite the chemistry of healing.

All this places us directly on stage with a giant of twentieth-century theater—Constantin Stanislavski. More about him in the next scene.

ACT NOW!

SCENE TWO

....

STANISLAVSKI SOLVES THE "PROBLEM OF EMOTION"

The findings of psychoneuroimmunology hold out exciting possibilities for us. In addition, they come with an implied task—an assignment, if you will.

If it's true that our feelings can affect our immunity and overall level of health, then it's urgent for us to work skillfully with feelings. This means observing our feelings, cultivating positive feelings, and releasing negative ones.

There's a problem here, and it's rarely mentioned in all the literature on psychoneuroimmunology. How do we create an emotional atmosphere that's conducive to health?

Psychoneuroimmunology suggests strongly that emotions play a role in healing. Yet it's surprising how often researchers in this field gloss over a common-sense fact: Feelings are difficult to summon at will.

In fact, feelings are fluid and fleeting. They often arise on their own for reasons we can't explain; they peak for a while and then mysteriously pass away. The question remains: How do we access healing feelings? How do we stimulate the inner chemistry of emotion—a chemistry that has healing potential?

Stanislavski spent a lifetime developing a method that would address what he called the "problem of emotions." And he knew it was based on the laws of nature.

Feelings— fluid and fleeting

The "problem of emotions" points us toward a central problem of human living—how to balance feeling, thought, and action. If you're like me, you go through periods where these three aspects of life get totally out of kilter.

For instance, I can think about getting up to jog at 5:30 a.m. and make grand plans to do so. But when the alarm goes off, my feelings speak louder than my thoughts.

"Don't get up," they plead. "Lingering in bed is one of the great pleasures of life. And you know that pleasure is good for your immune system, too. Just take it easy. You can exercise later." After a few minutes of that unassailable logic, my actions follow suit. I unplug the alarm clock and settle back into a blissful sleep.

Human beings have recognized this dilemma for thousands of years. Almost two thousand years ago, for example, Paul mentioned it in the Bible. "The good that I would do," said Paul, "I do not. And that which I want not to do—that I do." Here Paul points to a discrepancy between his thoughts (his intentions to do good) and his actions.

Just about anyone who's ever tried to quit smoking, lose weight, start an exercise program, or change another health-related habit has directly experienced what Paul wrote about. I would paraphrase Paul this way: If the feeling chemistry isn't "right," then thoughts and actions won't be right either.

The problem of emotions has several different slants, depending on the application. For actors, it is the problem of how to conjure up the chemical feelings of the characters they play. This is essential for producing spontaneous and convincing actions on stage.

If movie star Mel Gibson gets up on stage to play Hamlet, then he needs to feel grief, anger, doubt, fear, and all those emotions that make up the character we call Hamlet. But if Gibson is thinking only about the pastrami sandwich he had for lunch or about the cast party he's going to attend after the play, then he's probably not going to deliver a convincing performance. Gibson needs some way to access those powerful, complicated emotions that lead Hamlet to see ghosts and duel his adversaries to the death.

Before an audience can feel the emotions of actors, these artists must first create the chemistry of those feelings in themselves. For example, sad actors cannot authentically portray a happy feeling to an audience. Their act will simply not be believable.

For those of us interested in psychoneuroimmunology, the problem is how to arouse emotions that promote healing and immunity—not only for ourselves but for others. We want to regularly release the endorphins, T-cells, gamma globulins, and other chemicals and cells that protect us from disease and produce healthy doses of pleasure. And like actors, we find that feelings cannot be directly commanded. We cannot change feelings by concentrating on the chemistry of the feelings. We can change our feelings only by concentrating on altering our thoughts and actions.

ACT NOW!

Pavlov's dogs reveal some secrets of chemistry

So, there it is—the problem of emotion. How do we turn on the healing chemistry that comes with positive feeling? Fortunately, there is an answer to this question. Understanding that answer takes us to Saint Petersburg, Russia, during the early twentieth century.

Ivan Pavlov was one of the great physiologists of his time, a distinguished scientist at the University of Saint Petersburg who won a Nobel Prize in 1904. At one point in his career, Pavlov did a series of studies on digestion. In fact, Pavlov's most famous work—experiments that almost every student of physiology and psychology learns about—involved the digestive systems of dogs.

At one point in these studies, Pavlov fed dogs and then analyzed their salivary and stomach secretions. He was particularly interested in how the secretions were triggered. Eventually Pavlov posed a question: Is there something other than food that could stimulate my dogs to produce these digestive juices?

To find out, Pavlov started a new routine at feeding time. Every time he brought the dogs dishes of food, he rang a bell. After doing this for some time, he noticed that the dogs salivated when they heard the bell ring—*even though there was no food in their dishes.*

This may not sound like earth-shattering news. Yet Pavlov's dogs focused scientists' attention on conditioning—a concept that looms large in twentieth-century psychology. Pavlov's dogs had been *conditioned* to secrete digestive juices at the sound of a bell. What's more, these secretions were exactly the same fluids the dogs produced when they were actually eating.

In short, Pavlov discovered how to trigger a certain kind of chemistry. And in so doing, he brushed right up against the problem of emotion. Those of us who want to trigger the inner chemistry of positive health and healing may have something to learn from Dr. Pavlov's dogs.

Stanislavski meets Dr. Pavlov

News of Pavlov's work reached Moscow, where it gained the attention of a young man named Constantin Stanislavski. Though Stanislavski was an actor and a teacher of acting, we know that he read widely and was vitally interested in psychology and physiology. What's more, he constantly searched for ways to apply the discoveries of these sciences to the art of acting.

Here is where I can picture another legendary meeting taking place—much like the meeting I imagined between Descartes and the Pope. In my mind's eye, I see Stanislavski meeting Pavlov for coffee in a crowded Moscow cafe after one of Stanislavski's acting classes.

"You know, when I heard about what you were doing with those dogs back in Saint Petersburg, I got a little upset," Stanislavski would have said. "After all, it's kind of a dirty trick to make those poor dogs think they're going to get food and then just ring a bell in their faces. That's changing their chemistry by trickery. But you know, I got to thinking about what you're doing, and I started wondering whether I could do something with my acting students that's very much like what you're doing with your dogs.

"Now, I don't really want to make my students salivate at the sound of a bell," Stanislavski would have continued. "I don't even care what or when they eat. But I am interested in triggering a chemical and physical response in my students—an emotional response that will help them on stage.

"You see, my students say that on some nights they're really inspired, really 'on'—that the chemistry of the stage is just right for them and the audience. On those nights, they deliver good performances. On other nights, however, they don't even feel like walking on stage, let alone inspired to give a stellar performance. The feelings of inspiration that they depend on for their very livelihood are fleeting and unreliable."

"So you want to treat your students like dogs?" Pavlov asks. "Is that it?"

"Ha, ha—very perceptive!" says Stanislavski. "Here's my question for you, good Dr. Pavlov: How do we find a reliable way to trigger an 'on' performance? What is the chemistry of inspiration and how do we produce it? How can we access those powerful feelings that will move actors as individuals and our audiences in general to an emotional level, sending them home feeling glad they took part in the theater? I think your monumental discoveries can help me find some answers."

Again, I don't know whether such an exchange between these two men ever occurred. Yet in Stanislavski's mind there was a real exchange of ideas taking place, one that crossed the boundaries between physiology and acting.

Inviting inspiration— the aim of the "Method"

To understand how exciting this exchange was, remember that Stanislavski was a key player in the Moscow Arts Theatre. Russian theater at this time was one of the hot beds of theatrical performance and study, and Stanislavski eventually became its leader.

As a performer, director, and teacher, Stanislavski created a body of ideas that has influenced many of the great actors of our day. Today that body of ideas is known as the "Method school of acting," or simply the "Method."

In addition to teaching students in Moscow, Stanislavski brought his knowledge of the theater to the United States. Through Stanislavski's American students (including Lee Strasberg and Stella Adler of the Actor's Studio in New York City), the Method has played a vital role in American theater—stage, screen, and television. Dustin Hoffman, Marlon Brando, Robert DeNiro, James Dean, and Marilyn Monroe are just a few of the people who've studied and applied the Method.

Through the Method, Stanislavski wanted to help actors change their very physiology. He wanted them to access the chemistry of sadness, the chemistry of anger, the chemistry of happiness, and all the other feelings that made up the characters they played. Moreover, Stanislavski wanted his students to trigger those changes in chemistry at the exact moment that the feelings were called for on stage.

This is where the genius of the Method lies. Stanislavski found that feelings are a conditioned response. Just as Pavlov conditioned his dogs to produce a physical-chemical response, Stanislavski conditioned his students to produce an emotional-chemical response.

And the key, Stanislavski found, is to focus not on the desired emotion itself but on the antecedents of that emotion. By the word *antecedent*, Stanislavski meant all the things that happen before a certain feeling occurs, including:

- What we see

- What we hear

- How we place our attention

- What we picture in our minds

- What we say to ourselves

- What we say to others

- What we taste

- How we speak (including inflection, pitch, and tone of voice)

- How we gesture

- How we sit, stand, or walk

- How we breathe

- How we dress

- What we smell

If you study this list carefully, you'll notice that all its items relate either to thinking or action. As Stanislavski knew, we often determine someone's emotions by their motions—their posture and gestures. In addition, the Method implies that motion, thought, and emotion are all closely related. We could express this with another shorthand expression:

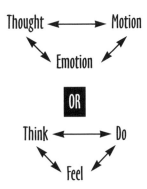

In effect, Stanislavski said: Don't worry about inspiration. Don't worry about what you feel. Just concentrate on the antecedents of a feeling—what you *think* about and what you *do*. Just work with thought and action and leave feelings to Mother Nature; she will produce them when she's ready. As you work in this way, you pave the way for changes in feeling that will echo through the very chemistry of your body. Eventually you will reach the state of feeling and inspiration you desire.

With these ideas, Stanislavski essentially solves the problem of emotion. In fact, Stanislavski often referred to the Method as "our emotion technique." How well he understood the importance of feeling and the means of accessing it.

Complicated yet simple

Stanislavski's Method is profound. At the same time, it echoes some everyday wisdom. Perhaps you've heard or even said the Serenity Prayer: "God, grant me the serenity to accept the things I cannot change, the courage to change the things I can, and the wisdom to know the difference."

· ·

I like to think of the Method as a direct application of these simple yet powerful ideas. Stanislavski knew that once a feeling chemistry is present, our only task is to experience it just as it is. We cannot directly change our feelings; they belong to that category of things we're called on to accept. Thoughts and actions, however, are a different matter; they belong to the category of things we *can* change.

In essence, the Method is a set of instructions for helping us remember the difference between these two categories—what we can't change and what we can change.

Stanislavski had another way of explaining this difference. He often spoke about a creative tension between the conscious and the subconscious. He applied the term *conscious* to those aspects of ourselves that we can change at will—our thoughts and actions. The word *unconscious* he reserved for the whole realm of feeling and physiology.

So, the Method is all about using the conscious to unleash the subconscious. In other words, the Method teaches us how to change our thoughts and our actions in a way that sets the stage for powerful feelings and a new physiology. We can learn how to act in a way that gets the feeling chemistry tuned up and turned on.

This is inspiration—getting in the spirit. Inspiration is the goal of the Method. When actors are inspired, said Stanislavski, they naturally and spontaneously act like the characters they portray. "A creative actor feels his own life in the life of his part," wrote Stanislavski in his book *An Actor Prepares*. In the state of inspiration, the body, mind, and soul of the actor become one with the body, mind, and soul of the character.

By the way, that word *prepares* is important. The Method does not manufacture inspiration. Indeed, inspiration is a mysterious gift that wells up from deep down inside us; it cannot be manufactured at will. Rather, the Method invites inspiration—it prepares us for new feelings and clears a path for new physiology.

Like all feelings, inspirational chemistry will come of its own accord once we set the stage for it with thoughts and actions that trigger it.

Stanislavski sets the stage

I call Stanislavski a genius because in many ways he was far ahead of his time. In the Method, we find seeds of many later disciplines, including psychoneuroimmunology and the whole field of alternative medicine.

Stanislavski also anticipated the whole field of cognitive-behavioral psychology—a branch of psychology with close ties to psychoneuroimmunology. Cognitive-behavioral psychology is another complex term we can understand by dividing it into parts. The word cognitive refers to thinking and *behavioral* refers to action.

According to cognitive-behavioral psychology, the path to changing human feeling lies in changing what we think and what we do. Here we come full circle, back to the very same antecedents of feeling that Stanislavski spoke about.

I could give you many examples of the common ground between cognitive-behavioral psychology and the Method. Let me cite just one. It comes from the writing of William Glasser in his book *Take Effective Control of Your Life*. In the passage below, Glasser repeats the same points about thinking, feeling, and action that Stanislavski made almost a half-century earlier:

> Right now, while reading this chapter, please try this simple experiment. Try to feel angry. Go to work at it and try to generate rage. You will probably find it

. . . .

impossible. . . . Even an actor has to have a reason (character motivation) before he can generate a feeling. Try as we will, it is almost impossible, arbitrarily, to choose a feeling that makes no sense.

Now try to think green; blot out all else and think only of the color green. This may be possible, but it takes a great deal of concentration. . . . Now raise your right hand—pick it up and raise it above your head. Immediately you see that this behavior is easy to accomplish because, as we have evolved, the doing component of our behavior has come almost completely under our voluntary control. . . .

At this stage of our evolution, we have almost total control over the doing component, some over the thinking component, almost none over the feeling component, and even less over the physiological component of our total behavior. . . . *Because we always have control over the doing component of our behavior, if we markedly change that component, we cannot avoid changing the thinking, feeling, and physiological components as well.*

Here Glasser echoes Stanislavski's teaching that the physiology of our feelings is largely linked to our thoughts and actions.

Before ending this chapter, I want to prevent one potential misunderstanding. After hearing about the Method for the first time, some people get confused. "Stanislavski is talking out of both sides of his mouth," they respond. "He seems to say that feelings cannot be commanded. Yet he gives us a whole body of techniques for commanding feelings."

. . . .

I can understand how people get this impression, so I want to be clear about this point. Yes, Stanislavski did teach that feelings cannot be *directly* commanded. But he also said that feelings can be *indirectly* invited through techniques of thought and bodily movement. To avoid confusion, just remember the distinction between *direct* control and *indirect* influence.

Stanislavski sometimes called the Method a "grammar of acting." I think we could expand that term and call it a "grammar of physical and mental health" as well. Through the teachings of Stanislavski we can not only enjoy the chemistry of superb theater but the chemistry of happiness and health as well. In a way, the Method is applied psychoneuroimmunology.

Included in the Method are valuable techniques for anyone who wishes to access the emotions associated with health and healing. We can start to develop the chemistry of healing by literally getting into the act—by thinking and behaving like healthy people. You'll read more about how to do this as you raise the curtain on the scenes that follow.

ACT NOW!

....

....

SCENE THREE

MORE ABOUT THE METHOD

Stanislavski addresses the "inner" actor

In order to appreciate the depth of Stanislavski's contribution, we must put him in the context of theater history.

Before Stanislavski came along, there was no "inner" method of acting. People who wanted to become actors concentrated on externals: enunciating, projecting the voice, gesturing, fencing, and developing strong, supple bodies.

According to this school of thought, actors did not really need to identify with or even sympathize with the characters they played. The main effort required of actors was *imitation*—carefully copying the speech, gestures, and mannerisms of their imagined characters. As to what those characters might have thought or felt—this was not an actor's real concern.

Of course, it is possible that some of these earlier actors did get into the chemistry of a part. Yet this was not the goal of their training.

ACT NOW!

Before Stanislavski, that training concentrated only on the outer trappings of a role.

Stanislavski's approach was almost the opposite. He placed great emphasis on the inner aspects of human feeling. He taught that thoughts as well as external objects and overt actions can trigger the chemistry of a desired emotion.

When it comes to explaining the difference between these two schools of acting, I like to quote the following passage. It was written by two physicians, Hillel Finestone and David Conter, and taken from their article, "Acting In Medical Practice":

> Roughly speaking, there are two broad approaches to developing a role. One—associated in our time most famously with the late Lord [Laurence] Olivier—moves from the outside in. That is, physical gestures, movements, facial and vocal expressions, are selected individually to compose an expressive whole. The external approach contrasts with the *inside-out approach*—typified perhaps by Marlon Brando—where the emphasis is on an actor creating within themselves the desired emotion, with the result that the *physical* expression will follow naturally.

That last sentence—which speaks about creating within yourself the desired emotion so that the expression follows naturally—gets to the core of the Method.

From forced feeling to natural emotion

Stanislavski stated that his Method of acting was not invented but was discovered in the laws of nature. His system was the result of a lifelong search for a method that would enable an actor to create the image of a character—embody a human spirit and portray it on stage with artistic beauty.

Our basic question is: Which of life's many emotions and roles do we most want to portray on our personal "stage"? Who do we strive to be?

Most of all, what chemistry, what physiology, do we want to act out?

There are many answers to that question, but some are most dominant: to improve our well-being, to experience pleasant emotions, to live a long, happy, healthy, and wealthy life. (For me, *wealth* refers not only to money but to psychic wealth as well.)

Human behavior revolves around avoiding pain or pursuing pleasure. Avoiding pain can be unpleasant hard work but the pursuit of pleasure is usually fun. Eliminating the negative is much harder to do than accentuating the positive. So we tend to enjoy generating the chemistry of good feeling. And people embark on a lifelong quest to feel good as much of the time as possible. Now the scientific field of psychoneuroimmunology is teaching that experiencing pleasant feelings may enhance our health. Hey, pleasant feelings are good for what ails us!

Yet this quest is flawed because it ignores a fundamental principle of human nature, something that Stanislavski would have called the problem of emotion. Feelings cannot be directly controlled. No amount of simple wishing can generate or change the chemistry of feelings. Rather, changes in feeling must first involve changes in thoughts and actions.

This fact lends an element of tragedy to life. Most human beings are involved in a fruitless attempt to command their feelings. They try to control what cannot be controlled and to fix what cannot be fixed by simply wishing it to happen. Unfortunately, many in our society lead feeling-centered lives.

Stanislavski saw this same tendency in his students. They, too, were primarily centered on feeling. When they first came to Moscow Arts Theatre for acting classes, many of the students walked on stage with one aim—a wish to arouse an emotional response in themselves and in the audience. As a result, they overacted.

When actors try to deliberately arouse a certain emotion in their audience, their efforts are bound to strike a false note unless they first develop the chemistry of that specific genuine emotion.

As Stanislavski often reminded his students, natural emotions arise effortlessly from given circumstances. We must not try so hard to create them. Instead, these emotions come of their own accord when we focus instead on proper thought, scripting, and acting. Helping students apply this insight was the aim and purpose of Stanislavski's Method.

Focus on attention, intention, and action

With this aim in mind, Stanislavski offered his students the daring suggestion to forget their feelings. He counseled them over and over again to stop striving for emotional extremes. He even told them to forget about inspiration. None of these can be controlled directly by wishing or wanting, he said. Instead, the great teacher advised, put all your energy into those aspects of life that you can control. Basically, these are attention, intention, and action.

Stanislavski counseled his students to lead a purpose-centered, action-centered life on—and off—stage. In addition, he reminded them to constantly pay attention not only to their actions and purpose, but to the scenery, props, and other people on stage. All we can do, Stanislavski said, is concentrate on these factors and let emotions come when they will.

You cannot force yourself or anyone else to feel the emotions of the character you play. These emotions must arise spontaneously. All you can do is clear a path for them, said Stanislavski. You can sow the seeds of inspiration through the three great factors of attention, intention, and action. When you do, the appropriate feelings will arise naturally and spontaneously in you and in your audience. As the saying goes, "Just let it happen!"

It so happens that this is great advice, not only for actors but for all of us.

Like students of acting, we too can focus on attention, intention, and action. At any given moment we can ask ourselves three questions:

- What am I paying attention to right now?

- What is my intention?

- What action can I take to achieve my intention?

Asking these questions reminds us of those things in life we can truly control. Answering them sets the stage for powerful emotion, positive chemistry, and health.

ACT NOW!

....

Try this acting experiment

To demonstrate this for yourself, try a short experiment. Right now, with no prior thought or bodily movement, feel overwhelmingly happy.

Now feel depressed.

Next, feel rage.

And now, feel inspired.

How did it go? If you failed to create anything resembling these four emotions, don't worry. You just proved the point of this experiment: Feelings cannot be manufactured by direct command—by wishing. This is a central insight for actors, who must portray a whole palette of emotions as the very basis of their profession.

Some people will object, "But wait, I *could* do it. I was able to produce those four feelings at will." If we question these people, we'll find that they did not directly manipulate their feelings. Instead, they probably focused their attention in a new way, decided to take a new action, or moved their bodies in a new way, even though they were instructed not to. In short, they changed their attention, intention, or action.

For example, the person who wants to feel happy can think about a pleasant memory or recall an inspirational quotation. He could make plans to do something pleasant, such as meeting a close friend for dinner. Or he could move like a happy person—straighten his posture, smile, laugh, or take a brisk walk to stimulate endorphin production.

The person who wants to feel sad can use similar strategies but in the opposite way. She can picture distressing scenes in her mind or repeat self-defeating phrases. (*I'll never be any good at this. The*

....

good things that happen to other people never seem to happen to me.) She can also think about all the items on her to-do list that she's dreading, such as cleaning the bathroom and washing windows. Or she could move her body in a depressing way—slumping her shoulders, contorting her face muscles into a frown, and avoiding eye contact with other people.

As you may remember from the prologue, researcher David Reynolds used such strategies so well that he successfully passed as a suicidally depressed patient in a mental hospital.

In both of the above examples, attention, intention, and action are what people changed. And in both cases, the desired feelings—the desired chemistry—resulted.

Stanislavski's Method gives new meaning to the suggestion, "Take control of your life." His discoveries point to what we can control (action, intention, and attention) and what we cannot (feeling). As Stanislavski knew, our moment-to-moment choices of attention, intention, and action create our lives. He saw this as a law of nature which we are called to obey if we want to act effectively. The same law can help us enjoy good health as well.

Acting is reincarnation

Stanislavski's theory was that actors need to "live" their parts. Their thoughts, actions, and feelings must become the thoughts, actions, and feelings of their characters.

During a successful performance, the actor and the character fuse to become one. The height of the actor's art is to say, "My life and my part merge," or "I walk my talk!" Stanislavski related that when one sensed this real kinship with the role, this newly created being "became soul of your soul and flesh of your flesh."

This presents a goal that seems almost impossible to achieve. In real life—life outside the theater—we are spontaneous. Our words and actions spring naturally from our feelings and intentions. But on stage, actors are called on to experience and portray emotions they have no reason to feel. How can they possibly live their parts?

How could Marlon Brando, for example, live the part of Stanley Kowalski, the swaggering, hard-drinking seducer of women in a *Streetcar Named Desire*? Kowalski was a fictional character who lived only in the mind of playwright Tennessee Williams. What's more, Kowalski presumably had an outlook on life and a set of emotions that were totally different than Brando's. How could Marlon Brando "give birth" to Stanley Kowalski?

This is the question that Stanislavski raised and answered. His goal was to create a method that allowed people to think, feel, and act as their characters would—and to do all this on stage as spontaneously as in real life. Stanislavski called this result inspiration, and his Method was the means to achieve it.

The Method, he said, aimed "to create the life of a human soul and render it in artistic form." There's another way to say this: Acting is reincarnation.

Using the Method, an actor conceives and gives birth to a new human being—the character she portrays. While on stage, an actor *becomes* someone else. Or, more accurately, her thoughts, feelings, and actions merge with those of the character.

When this happens, the character ceases to be just a series of lines in a play script. Instead, the character comes to life in the body, mind, and soul of the actor. If maintained over time, the feeling chemistry of that character changes the actor into something new. And the character becomes real.

Stanislavski was not afraid to call this process reincarnation. He was not dabbling in Eastern religion or the occult; instead, he was describing what happens when a character comes alive on stage. Actress Sonia Moore, who studied with Stanislavski, explained it this way:

> There is nothing mystical, no mysterious transformation, in the Stanislavski reincarnation. An actor achieves reincarnation when he achieves the truthful behavior of the character, when his actions are interwoven with words and thoughts, when he has searched for all the necessary traits of a character, when he surrounds himself with its given circumstances and becomes so accustomed to them that he does not know where his own personality leaves off and that of the character begins. Stanislavski considered reincarnation the height of the actor's art.

The rest of us can reach dramatic heights through reincarnation, too. This act may be the ultimate alternative medicine.

In essence, Stanislavski said, focus your attention as your character would. Know your character's intentions. And know your character's typical gestures and movements. When these three things come to the forefront of your mind, then genuine feeling and inspiration will arise by themselves. You will actually incarnate a new human being—the character you are portraying.

Well, if actors can do this, why not you and me? We don't have to move through life playing the same stale parts and speaking the same tired, often sick, lines.

If we are not content with the parts we play on the stage of everyday life, then we can walk on to a new stage and play a new part.

ACT NOW!

By changing our focus of attention, intention, and action, we, too, can give birth to a new human being—the healthy person we desire to be. We, too, can unleash the healing chemistry of our pharmacy within.

This is the meaning and power of the Method for all of us. Gaining access to this powerful inner chemistry takes us into some specific guidelines for attention, intention, and action.

Guidelines for attention

"Observe! Observe!" I can imagine Stanislavski shouting this word repeatedly to acting students whose attention wavered on stage. Constant observation is part of the actor's essential tool kit. The actor must be aware of what's taking place on stage—what the other characters are saying, doing, thinking, and feeling; the placement of props; the play of light and shadow; and any other sensory details significant to the action on stage. Without this awareness, an actor's speech and movements will be inappropriate to the given circumstances of the play.

Observation is also essential for those of us who occupy the stage of everyday life. We, too, can learn to pay attention to the sensory details of our environment—sights, sounds, colors, textures, tastes, smells. We can carefully observe our thoughts, feelings, sensations, and movements. When we bring all this data into awareness, we're more truly aware of what's happening in, upon, and around us. Our actions can then be much more appropriate and on target.

Observing the external world has a special advantage: It takes our mind off ourselves. Unhappy people often focus their attention exclusively on themselves, asking: What's good for me? How will this benefit me? What's in it for me? What do I want? How can I benefit? In short, they become self-centered, with thoughts turned inward. This results in the toxic dump" of chemical unhappiness.

Happy people, on the other hand, are "out-going," willing to go beyond themselves. Their "you-uniqueness" lies in how they talk and think about you, we, and us. These people concentrate on how they affect others rather than on how others affect them. They ask: What can I do for others? How can I contribute? Given the circumstances I find myself in right now, how can I help? They know that caring for others is one of the best ways we can care for ourselves.

Like successful actors, these people collaborate toward shared goals. They don't try to steal the show by acting in an I-centered way. Instead, they become "we" thinkers and interact with their cast and audience to let out a chemical emotion of cooperation and success.

Take the word *llness*. Doesn't look like much of a word, does it? However, people with outgoing actions and thoughts add *we* to the front of this word—and it becomes *wellness*. In contrast, those who dwell in self-centered "I" thinking add an *i*, and the word becomes *illness*.

 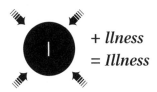

Perhaps the chemical differences between illness and wellness relate to to some degree to the difference between *I* and *we*, between inward or outward thinking, between the unhappiness of going in or the happiness of focusing out.

There's a Japanese saying: "Self-centeredness is suffering." When we widen our focus of attention through service and contribution to others, we take the focus off ourselves and widen our circle of attention to embrace others. The result is often a major shift in feeling chemistry. The feeling is good. And good chemistry contributes to health-happiness.Where we place our attention, then, has a lot to do with our health and happiness. Think about how different people focus their attention while reading a daily newspaper.

One person's attention is drawn to all the stories of war, rape, or violence. He believes that the world is basically unsafe, and he pays attention only to the stories that confirm that belief.

Another person turns to the sports page, the TV listings, the comics, and feature stories that focus on acts of kindness. This person sees the world as largely a safe place, one to be enjoyed. Her style of reading the newspaper reflects that belief. These two people may live in the same city, but emotionally they occupy two totally different worlds.

In short, our attention creates our world. If we focus on the beauty around us, our lives will take on a corresponding lightness and expansiveness. If we focus only on the ugliness of our circumstances and the meanness of others, then our world contracts and dims. In other words, "We see what we see, and the me I see is the me I'll be!"

Fortunately we can learn to control our attention. Following are some guidelines for training attention, as suggested by Stanislavsk.

Wake up to the present moment

One of Stanislavski's favorite sayings was "today, here, now." This reminds actors to focus their attention on the present moment. After all, the chemistry of every performance is different. Each night, the audience is different. Each day, the other players change their approach to portraying their characters. If actors go on stage each night with the same canned gestures and mannerisms, their performance will be stale, lifeless, and off-key.

In the same way, we can feel more alive when we wake up to the present moment. When eating, for example, we can take time to eat with mindfulness and full awareness. We can slow down to savor each bite, to enjoy the texture, taste, and aroma of our food. When we eat slowly and with full attention, we may find that we eat less and enjoy our meals even more.

Even during our most harried days, we can practice this kind of exquisite attention in the midst of almost any activity—while walking, listening to music, preparing meals, playing with children, working, gardening, or doing household chores. This is a potent way to maximize enjoyment, manage stress, and weather even the most down performances in our daily lives.

Choose your circle of attention

We often speak of a point of attention. Yet attention also has the qualities of a circle, including radius and circumference. For example, the circle of your attention could be wide enough so you're aware of what's taking place in a large ballroom. It could be small enough to notice only what's on the tip of your nose. Or your circle of attention could fall anywhere between these extremes.

Stanislavski urged his students to constantly notice and adjust their circle of attention. There's an important reason for this suggestion. When an actor's attention wanders and she starts thinking about some event taking place offstage, then communication between the actors breaks down. Her circle of attention is too wide, and she loses touch with the events of the play.

One way she can "wake up" and rivet her attention back on stage is to shrink her circle of attention. For example, she could narrow her attention to a single prop, such as a lamp or table. She could also place her circle of attention on another actor's face or costume.

This advice has universal application: Anyone of us can ask at any moment, "How wide is my circle of attention right now? In order to do anything well, we must find an appropriate circle of attention for that activity.

If you're supervising 10 children on a large playground, for instance, then a fairly wide circle of attention is called for. But when you're listening sympathetically to a close friend who's on the verge of tears, then it's wise to shrink your attention so it encircles only the person in from of you.

An example from my own experience come to mind. When I was Peace Corps doctor in Ethiopia, I directed a large immunization clinic. Early in a typical day my focus of attention was broad, embracing a throng of patients and my assisting staff. However, later in the day my attention was concentrated to the "cutting edge," focused on one patient in the operating room for the removal of a ruptured appendix. In the immunization clinic my attention was diffuse; in surgery, I needed to be sharply focused.

Communication between people is often lost for the simple reason that their circles of attention never meet. Their attention is easily distracted; their circles shrink and expand almost by accident. When this happens, people no longer share the same stage. They are no longer present for one another. No real communion between them can take place. The solution is to take conscious control of our circle of attention.

Store and recall impressions

Actors are called on to create an infinite variety of emotional states. They are asked to see into the hearts of many characters, to penetrate the very essence of their thoughts and the chemistry of their feelings. Achieving these goals calls for constant and precise observation of the external world.

Actors must absorb the finest details of the objects and events that make up ordinary circumstances. In addition, they must be astute observers of people. They must observe how people walk, sit, stand, and perform the tasks of daily life. They must see into the minds and hearts of people with almost omniscient power. All these sensory impressions—everything they touch, taste, smell, hear, and see—will become the raw materials for creating characters both onstage and offstage.

Stanislavski's suggestion has a basis in science. Modern brain research indicates that all of our sensory impressions are recorded and chemically stored, much like a vast interior videotape.

In one series of experiments, neurosurgeon Wilbur Penfield used electrodes to stimulate certain areas of his subjects' brains. Under this kind of stimulation, many of the subjects reported that they not only remembered past events but relived them in vivid detail—down to the smallest detail of sight, sound, smell, taste, and touch.

Besides recalling the details of such events, these subjects re-experienced the *emotions* they connected with these events. When it comes to memory, it seems, nothing is lost. Perhaps all of our experiences and memories are available to us if we can only access them.

Here again, Stanislavski was ahead of his time. Decades before Penfield's experiments took place, Stanislavski told his students they possessed an emotional memory. What's more, he taught them to access this store of emotional impressions and continually add to it through careful observation.

Each of us possesses a rich bank of emotional memories. Many of these memories are built around subtle clues that are only seen

....

with the chemistry of the subconscious mind. We can learn to observe and identify these chemical triggers that are usually called gut feelings or intuition.

What's more, we can withdraw from this emotional bank account at any time. When lonely, we can relive a time when we felt loved. When depressed, we can recall a time when we felt powerful and alive.

All states of mind are available to us at any moment. By training ourselves to store and recall impressions, we can change the texture of our feelings in a moment.

Observe yourself

Stanislavski maintained that skilled actors must constantly observe themselves. Even when an actor fully reincarnates a character, he or she should observe himself or herself playing that character, much as the audience does. Indeed, actors must do this to judge the quality of their performance and change what isn't working on- (or off-) stage.

Like skilled actors, people who enjoy profound states of health are usually astute self-observers. They can describe their current health habits in great detail. And if they do get sick, these people can give precise descriptions of their symptoms. All this data makes for accurate diagnosis and effective treatment. Often small changes, even minute adjustments of behavior or thinking, are all that's needed to trigger the desired feeling chemistry.

Notice beauty

As I mentioned earlier, Stanislavski's concept of emotional memory means that all of us carry inside a rich store of feeling. In partic-

....

ular, said Stanislavski, scenes of natural beauty have the power to arouse strong feelings and pleasant associations. Stanislavski advised his acting students to notice beauty in their everyday surroundings and to seek out places of great natural beauty. Doing so gave them a broader base of memories to draw upon when acting.

Any of us who want to play a happy, healthy role can apply the same advice. If we want to experience the positive chemistry of healing emotions, then we can arrange our homes and offices with beauty and aesthetics in mind. We can notice how the look and feel of our daily environments affect our feelings.

Observe ugliness

Stanislavski understood that we recognize beauty only in contrast to what we find ugly. The same idea of contrast applies to any experience: We know wetness only in contrast to dryness, happiness in contrast to sadness, and so on.

Remembering this, we can open up to the whole range of our experience. Sigmund Freud and succeeding psychologists have testified to the danger of repressing or denying unpleasant emotions and painful memories. When it's appropriate, healthy people are willing to be uncomfortable. They are willing to tell the truth, even when doing so makes them squirm.

For example, most physicians who treat chemical dependency will tell you treatment really begins when alcoholics or addicts finally *admit* their lives have spun out of control. And treatment really begins to take hold when these people list their resentments and fears, when they admit how they've harmed others by drinking or drugging and become willing to make amends. Opening up to the unpleasant and even painful parts of their experience clears a path for healing and change. In this case, the act of making amends invites the chemistry of happiness and health.

ACT NOW!

· ·

Guidelines for intention

What do I want? There's power for all of us in asking this simple question. Yet many people fail to even raise this question, let alone answer it. It's no wonder, then, that in life they seldom get what they want.

We can avoid this problem by asking some powerful questions: What is my mission in life? What are my values? What projects are most worthy of my time and talents? Given the fact that my days are numbered, how shall I spend those days? How shall I rehearse the role I want to play? The very moment we ask such questions, we stop being victims of circumstance. By knowing what we want and taking action to produce it, we take charge of our lives.

All these are questions of *intention*. Stanislavski often spoke about the need for actors to know the intentions of their characters. And again, he made suggestions that apply with equal force to actors and non-actors alike.

Successful actors envision what they want to happen on opening night. They plan. They rehearse. They see the bright lights and anticipate the excitement of seeing the curtain rise. As explained by Steven Covey in *The Seven Basic Habits of Highly Effective People,* these actors become proactive; they "begin with the end in mind."

Plan your life

To portray a character convincingly, an actor must know what a character fundamentally wants. What's more, the actor must grasp the series of individual actions that leads characters to ultimately get what they want.

Stanislavski called the character's fundamental intention a *super-objective*—a goal. And he called the series of actions leading to the

· ·

super-objective the *through line of action*—the steps needed to reach the goal.

Translated into everyday language, choosing a super-objective and a through line of action is the same as identifying a goal and developing a plan of action. Many of us plan a day, a week, or a month ahead. Those of us who are bolder even set goals for the next quarter or year.

Stanislavski urged his students to go much further. He asked them to define the shape of a character's entire lifetime, to know what their characters want months, years, and even decades beyond the present. Actors can plan how they want to be remembered after the curtain falls. In the same way, we can ask how we want our "act" to be remembered—what we want our epitaph to say when the curtain falls on our earthly lives.

Students of Stanislavski often spent hours creating biographies of their characters. In addition, they plotted their characters' through line of action into the future. Only when knowing a character's intentions, both short- and long-range, can actors convincingly play those characters.

In the same way, each of us can take more effective action today when we have a clear picture of what we want one month, one year, or one decade from today. Stanislavski's goal was to help actors be perfectly spontaneous onstage and still act in line with their super-objective. Our lives can operate in a similar way. When we're clear about our overall objective in life, we can spontaneously create actions that lead to our goals.

The analogy to health is striking here. If we are going to play the part of a vigorous person at age 80 or 90, we must get our act together throughout life with sound health practices. We must set the stage of tomorrow—today.

ACT NOW!

Express your intentions effectively

As Stanislavski was fond of saying, no one does anything "in general." He knew that vagueness frustrates creativity and makes it impossible for an actor to portray a character with conviction.

For this reason, Stanislavski urged acting students to plan concrete, specific actions on stage. It is not enough, he said, to know that your character accepts his fate with resignation. This is far too general. Instead, you must know exactly what your character does to express that sense of resignation. For example, "The character stops talking, casts his eyes downward, slouches forward in his chair, and whimpers a barely audible cry."

Stanislavski insisted that actors name their objectives precisely, beginning with an active verb. Active verbs are those that point to actions we can observe. Shuffle, slouch, pout, whisper, walk, run, jog, call, drive, laugh, and cry are all examples of active verbs. Passive verbs such as is, feels, and seems inspire little in the way of action. For that reason, they are far less useful to actors, who must move on stage.

We need to use active verbs when expressing our intentions. For example, at one point my super-objective was to be a physician. That's fine as a starting point but hardly enough to inspire an effective through line of action.

To achieve this objective, I planned a series of actions beginning with active verbs: apply to medical school, take chemistry courses, read anatomy texts, memorize the names of muscle groups, and many more. Only when I could express my intentions in this way was it possible to turn my super-objective from a hazy ideal to a concrete reality.

Remember that less is more

Cut 80 percent! Stanislavski was fond of using this expression with students who overacted on stage. Mechanical acting involves doing far more than is needed to establish the reality of the character.

When an actor overacts, she simply does too much—says too much, gestures too much, and moves too much. When Stanislavski saw this happening, he advised students to be far more efficient. "Cut 80 percent" meant, "Give me only the essential actions—those I need to believe that you've really taken on the life of your character. Anything more than that is wasted."

Stanislavski's advice to cut 80 percent can also help us focus on what's truly important on the stage of daily life. In time management literature, you'll read about the 80/20 rule—the idea that 80 percent of the value of any to-do list is derived from only 20 percent of the items on that list. The suggestion here is to know your super-objective and then take only the actions needed to accomplish that objective.

Concentrating on the top 20 percent of your action items will most likely help you reach your goal more quickly than trying to accomplish all the action items on your list. With a firm purpose in mind, we can cut unnecessary activities from our lives, free up time, and still meet our goals more quickly.

This leads to a series of questions that can transform our approach to time. When planning, we can ask: How many of my activities truly serve me? What actions and commitments could be cut from my life with no loss of fulfillment or purpose on my part?

Try this exercise:

• Write out a to-do list of 10 items for today—10 specific actions you'd like to accomplish before going to bed tonight.

ACT NOW!

- Now assume that you only have time to do two of them. That's right—just two.

- With your super-objective in mind, what two items would you pick?

- Plan now to do these two items before doing anything else on your list.

- At the end of the day, evaluate how well you fulfilled your overall objectives in life merely by getting the two most essential items on your list done.

Next, think about what might happen if you did this consistently, day after day. Perhaps you could routinely purge items from your to-do lists and still accomplish what's most important to you. You might experience a life that is more fulfilling, more "on purpose," and less rushed. The secret is holding your super-objective firmly in mind and ruthlessly cutting out all actions that fail to serve it.

As you do some of the important items over and over again, they will become second nature—a habit and natural part of your act. When that happens, you can replace these items with new candidates for your 10 "most wanted" list.

One note before we move on to guidelines for action: There are no absolutes in theater, and most principles have exceptions. This is true of the "cut 80 percent" principle. While "less is more" is often a useful guideline for planning, there are times when "more is better."

When learning a new habit (rehearsing a new part), we may need to exaggerate a chosen attitude or action. For example, when working to retrain my posture, I often exaggerated the proper movements. Every few minutes for a stated period each day, I made a big act of straightening my spine and sitting or standing erect. Once I established a generally effective posture, I could "back off" and decrease my rehearsal periods by 80 percent.

Guidelines for action

There is an irony built into Stanislavski's ideas. On the one hand, he taught that the path to powerful acting is entering into the emotional life, the very chemistry, of a character.

When actors feel the feelings of their characters in their own hearts, they reach a state of inspiration. And when actors are inspired, they spontaneously speak, gesture, and move in ways that tell us they've actually become their characters. We can sum all this up in a single sentence: *Character produces action.*

Yet Stanislavski also taught that emotions cannot be controlled by simply "wishing." Emotions and inspiration are fickle, fleeting, and impermanent. All we can do is lay the groundwork for a desired emotional chemistry by paying detailed attention to a character's thoughts and actions.

When actors speak, gesture, and move in ways that are appropriate for their characters, then they start to feel the emotions of their characters. In short, action produces character. Emotion creates motion, and motion creates emotion.

Though these ideas seem contradictory, they are in fact complementary. Skilled actors hold both ideas in balance. The relationship between character and action, between feeling and movement, is circular. It's true that our feelings lead us to act in certain ways. But it's also true that our actions leads us to feel in certain ways.

Stanislavski had another name for this idea. He called it the *method of physical action.* I can imagine him saying to his students at the Moscow Arts Theatre:

> Forget inspiration. Forget your feelings. Just throw your whole effort into action. Know your character's super-objective, thoughts, and through-line of

action. Attend to these things and you will find that feelings take care of themselves. By taking on a character's actions, you'll begin to feel what the character feels. This lays the groundwork for an inspired performance."

This advice from Stanislavski implies the following suggestions.

Focus on action, not feeling

For actors, the method of physical actions is a lifesaver. It means that they don't have to *feel* inspired before they walk on stage.

Imagine a woman who's agreed to play Juliet in Shakespeare's famous play. One night, just an hour before her evening's scheduled performance, she calls her director and says, "Listen, I don't think I can play Juliet tonight. My boyfriend just dumped me, and right now I wouldn't give you a nickel for any of the male members of our species. And, by the way, that includes our precious Romeo. You can just find someone else to be Juliet tonight! I'll come back to work when I feel like playing Juliet again."

Admittedly, this is an extreme example. Yet it points out a common tendency. Many of us fall into the habit of waiting until we feel "right" before we take an effective action. We put off exercising until that magic day when we feel like exercising. We put off changing jobs because we just don't feel up to it.

Years ago, many of the people who opposed racially integrating our schools used a similar line of reasoning. "You cannot legislate feelings," they argued. Their implication was this: "We cannot integrate the schools until we feel comfortable with people of other races." They wanted feelings to take precedence over legislative action. As Will Rogers said, "Don't introduce me to that person. I can't go on hating someone I know."

Comments like these mire us again in the problem of emotion. Here are Stanislavski's own words on the subject:

> It would be wonderful if we could achieve a permanent method of repeating successful emotional experiences. But feelings cannot be fixed. They run through your fingers like water. That is why, whether you like it or not, it is necessary to find more substantial means of affecting and establishing your emotions.

Stanislavski's solution to this problem was the method of physical actions. This principle reminds me of an old saying: "Lead with the body and the mind will follow." For our purposes, I'll modify that saying a little: "Lead with actions and your feelings will follow."

In other words, start exercising and eventually you will *feel* like exercising. Start smiling and eventually you will *feel* happier. Start introducing yourself to people and soon you will *feel* like making new friends. Write 10 thank-you notes and eventually you will *feel* thankful. Spend time with people of different races and you will feel the value of integration.

In each case, you take constructive action first and allow the feeling to follow in its own time. As the field of psychoneuroimmunology indicates, mind, emotions, and body are one. Change one element in this equation and others will follow suit.

In her book *Improvisation for the Theater*, Viola Spolin expressed this idea in a colorful way. "When I laugh, my elbow laughs." This was her way of saying that any feeling echoes throughout the whole body.

When you laugh, you do more than move your mouth in a certain way; you may also move your elbows, hands, and even your feet in a way that's all your own. The chemistry of a feeling reacts in the whole body. You feel it in your gut, your head, in your heart—in every cell.

Every thought, mood, and intention is expressed through a certain action. By choosing to move, gesture, and speak in specific ways, actors can recreate the emotional lives of their desired character. And then their actions on stage will become spontaneous and true to the playwright's intention. This, in essence, is the method of physical action that Stanislavski taught. We can apply the same principle when seeking to influence our feeling chemistry and our health!

Choose the tempo-rhythm of your actions

Another term that Stanislavski liked to use was *tempo-rhythm*. Musicians are familiar with both of these words. They know that the same notes played at different speeds (tempo) and for different lengths of time (rhythm) will produce markedly different emotional responses in listeners. Dancers, too, know about tempo-rhythm. This knowledge guides them to choose long, slow, sweeping, and graceful movements when portraying relaxation and short, rapid, erratic movements when portraying excitement or fear.

Where tempo-rhythm is concerned, all of us are actors and musicians. Our bodies are instruments that we must keep in tune. Our actions have characteristic speeds and lengths, depending on our feelings in a given moment. And, as the method of physical action suggests, we can change the pace of our feelings by changing the pace of our actions.

The implied suggestion is to manage the tempo and rhythm of your attention, speech, and action. For example, to relax, imagine you're on film and about to enter a slow motion sequence. Deliberately slow down your movements. Breathe more slowly and deeply.

Lower the pitch of your voice and elongate your words. Then notice the change in your feelings. "Smile, breathe, and slow down" is a useful reminder for any time that we feel rushed or stressed.

A final word

In *An Actor Prepares*, Stanislavski wrote that everything in his teaching revolved around three principles: the super-objective (goal), the through line of action (direction), and the inner creative mood (also called the state of inspiration). He urged his students to focus on what arouses the inner chemistry of feeling. Think of the goal and direction that leads to this creative mood. In short, focus on what can be consciously controlled (thoughts and actions). This will lead you to the subconscious—the chemistry of a desired feeling.

ACT NOW!

....

....

More About the Method

INTERMISSION

SEVEN ASSUMPTIONS ABOUT ACTING, HEALING, AND FEELING

At this point, I'd like us to take a little break. If you've read the chapters straight through so far, you've probably been introduced to some new terms and definitions. You might even feel overwhelmed with new ideas. If so, take advantage of this short intermission to catch your breath.

This section marks a transition point in your reading. So far, you've read about a lot of ideas. Those ideas have been about psychoneuroimmunology, acting, Stanislavski, and the Method. The remaining chapters in this book move from theory to practice.

In the pages that follow, I offer specific suggestions for applying the ideas discussed in the first three chapters. Right now, I'll distill the major ideas from those early chapters into a short list of seven points I'd like you to remember. Take a deep breath, stretch, and read over this list a time or two before moving on. Then consider developing a new "opening show" and stage a plan for improved health and happiness.

....

1. We can act as if the mind-body connection is a fact.

Please remember that *Act Now* is not primarily about psychoneuroimmunology or even about acting. I am not out to make you a professional actor or a biochemist who can use scientific terms to describe how the mind and body connect. (In reality, the two have never been separated.)

But like an actor, you can experience the chemistry of happy emotions, health, and healing. I cannot prove that acting will cure illness, nor can I prove that acting techniques will make you feel good most of the time. But my intuition and gut chemistry tell me that acting techniques can help us give the healthy performance of a lifetime—for a lifetime. So instead of trying to prove psychoneuroimmunology, let's choose to act as if this claim is true and see what difference it makes in our lives.

My real purpose in *Act Now* is to entice you and our society into a new way of thinking about health. I've worked in the field of health education for years, both in one-on-one work with patients and as a speaker and seminar leader on this topic. Often I've struggled with the question of how to present health education as the vitally important topic that it is.

Too much health education amounts to preaching to the converted. Perhaps you know the scene: A speaker on health arrives during a corporate lunch. The audience consists of 20 well-conditioned people eating salads and drinking fruit juice. (On nice days, the audience shrinks because half the group will be outside exercising.) For the most part, this audience already knows what the speaker has to say.

While health education programs of this kind have value, they often fail to reach the people who need them the most. In my quest

....

to "jazz up" this whole field of health education and enlarge our audience, I've resorted to comedy, magic tricks, and other theatrical stunts. I aim to entertain my audiences and convince them that health education can be fun. My goal is to encourage more amateurs to walk on stage of the "health theater" and act healthy—and become a pro at acting well.

Today I'm most excited by the possibility of helping actors, healthcare providers, and health educators learn from each other. I want to catalyze a cooperative effort that will encourage people in the medical arts to think dramatically and people in the dramatic arts to think medically.

As I result, I foresee a new health paradigm, an alternative and complementary medicine called Act Well. It combines the best of western mainstream medicine and the best of the alternative healing concepts. Method acting, I believe, is an unheralded alternative medicine approach that can complement and enhance our approach to health care.

When this happens, I believe we'll see the teachings of health/wealth/happiness and psychoneuroimmunology reach a greatly expanded audience—not just of the healthy and those interested in health education, but of the unhealthy and uninterested as well. And this large, enthusiastic audience will encompass all social, economic, and ethnic groups.

And at the Health Education Theater a new stage will be set and an understandable script will be used to help performers act out the chemistries that accentuate the pos"I"tive. The director will teach the simple, new metaphor of Method acting—a method that will convey how easy it is to act well.

People who would never recite affirmations or go to cognitive-behavioral therapy might be willing to talk about writing themselves a new script or rehearsing new health habits—particularly when they learn that stars of stage, screen, and television use acting techniques to trigger the chemistry of a part. This approach will be of special benefit to the health educators of our youth. Learning how to act well should not be taught only in high school and college drama departments. The drama department should become part of the health education faculty.

Act Now is merely a prologue—the first scene in what I hope will be a long-running production about the connections between theater, feelings, healing, health, and happiness. My next book, *Act Too*, will chronicle these connections through interviews with actors about the specific techniques they use—techniques you can use to "see the stars."

2. Feelings are chemistry.

There are a number of biochemicals and cells that enhance the human immune system and protect us from illness. Among them are neuropeptides (including endorphins), macrophages, T–cells, N–cells, serotonin, melatonin, and gamma globulins. And many of these chemicals are associated with emotions.

Endorphins, for example, can produce states of relaxation, pleasure, and even euphoria. Likewise, feelings such as fear and anxiety often involve sudden rushes of adrenalin and other chemicals called cortisols. These substances originally helped our distant ancestors flee wild animals and other situations of physical danger.

Endorphins in particular have struck the "fancy" of the non-scientific community. The term *endorphins* has come to encompass the whole field of psychoneuroimmunology for most people. One reason the endorphins have caught on is that their structure is similar to morphine. We can understand how a morphine-like chemical can be called an "inner upper" that can get us high on life. How can we evoke a morphine-like chemical when we act well and "live it up"?

I assume that feelings and chemistry are largely the same. (In fact, I often use the terms *emotion, feeling,* and *chemistry* synonymously.) Change your emotional state, and you're bound to see changes in your body chemistry as well. Likewise, change your body chemistry, and you'll probably feel different feelings.

The chemicals we study in psychoneuroimmunology make up a "pharmacy" within us, a store of inner medication that can be as potent and effective as any medication we buy. And the great thing about this pharmacy is that it's open 24 hours a day.

We have a prescription for this pharmacy that says *"prn,"* meaning it can be filled anytime we want. Moreover, this "feel good" medication has no adverse side effects and is available to us free of charge, provided we know how to access our pharmacy. We have to learn the right moves—those almost magical techniques for positively changing our biochemistry. That's where a knowledge of acting can help us.

3. *Pleasure can heal.*

Some emotions may help us heal. For the most part, I assume these are the emotions like happiness, love, hope, joy, pleasure, satisfaction, optimism, and so on. My premise is that good feelings promote good healing. Pleasant feelings are the biochemicals that enhance our immune system.

In making this assumption, there are several things I am not saying.

For example, I am not saying that all pleasure is healthy. As we know from conditions like alcoholism and other drug addictions, some pleasures can be taken so far that they become destructive, both to ourselves and others. The healthy pleasures I want to promote are those that make for long-term health for you and for the rest of us as well. If an attitude or action feels good and harms no one, then why not do more of it and infuse your part on life's stage with a little more inspiration besides?

4. *Health means managing our states.*

For thousands of years, members of the healing profession have struggled to define the word *health.* Just about any medical dictionary I pick up hedges on this word—and for good reason. Health involves a delicate balance and harmony among scores of systems in the body-mind. The conventional notion of health as "the absence of disease" just doesn't do justice to this dramatic new idea.

I'd like to offer a working definition of health, one that does not describe the workings of the body-mind but focuses instead on what healthy human beings do: Max Dixon, a dramatic arts coach and member of the National Speakers' Association, suggests that we should become more aware of and monitor our state (of health) on the stages of our daily lives. Health means managing your states. By state I mean the sum total of all your mental and physical processes at any given moment.

This definition does justice to everyday reality. Healthy people, after all, sometimes get sick. Healthy people experience stress, fear, depression, and anxiety from time to time. What's more, some of the healthiest people you meet may have a disability.

If absolute freedom from mental and physical disease is not the mark of health, then what is? What distinguishes a healthy person is the ability to notice states, choose new states, and take action to change states.

When a healthy person experiences stress, for example, she detects that fact almost immediately. She may even say it out loud: "Wow! I'm really stressed out today," or "I'm really in a lousy state!" Next, she reminds herself that stress need not be a permanent state of body and mind. Finally, she has at her disposal some well-rehearsed strategies for reducing stress—often by changing her thoughts and actions in ways that accentuates the positive rather than trying to eliminate the negative.

The strategies for changing states differ from person to person. What's most important is we monitor our states and mount an appropriate response. The state we're in depends on the state of our chemistry. Make it a happy state.

5. Acting helps us manage our states.

In my definition of health we find a major connection between acting and healing. Skilled actors monitor their mental, emotional, and physical states on stage, sometimes moment by moment. In addition, they learn strategies to choose and change states so that they stay in character for the role they're playing.

As Stanislavski knew, some of our states are more subject to conscious control than others. We can direct our mental state (thoughts) and physical state (actions) much more easily than our emotional state (feelings). When seeking to change our health, then, it makes most sense to focus on our thoughts and actions. As we do, our feelings will gradually take care of themselves.

Today I consider Stanislavski to be one of the patron saints of medicine. I didn't study Stanislavski when I was in medical school. In fact, I didn't learn about Stanislavski until I'd practiced medicine for many years and begun to study the connections between the human mind and the body. But the more I observed the apparent relationship between happiness and health, the more I became convinced that this great benefactor of theater could become a key figure in medical history as well.

One more point. I'm not presenting the Stanislavski Method in detail—the way a student of the theater would learn it. The Method as taught to professional actors is highly technical and full of specific exercises to be played out on stage.

What's more, people understand the Method differently, depending on whether they choose to concentrate on the early or later, more evolved teachings of Stanislavski. For our purposes here, I'm presenting only those aspects of the Method that I see as most relevant to promoting health among nonactors like you and me.

Above all, I see acting as a metaphor that gives us a fresh, useful way to talk health—one that's accessible to many people. The language of the theater gives us a down-to-earth terminology for talking about the sometimes far out discoveries of psychoneuroimmunology. The Theater of Health offers its productions to old and young, rich and poor, educated and uneducated alike.

6. *It is OK to act.*

Perhaps you've said it of someone you know: "He's always on stage." Right! So are you and I. Each of us plays many different roles and occupies many "stages" during the course of a single day.

Our homes are one kind of stage, featuring our family members as key players. Then many of us walk on to a new stage at work, sharing the marquee with our cast of coworkers. (By the way, it's no accident that our worksite evaluations are called performance reviews.)

Each stage calls us to play a different role. We may find marked differences in the characters we play—perhaps confident and assertive at home but shy and retiring at the office. We're sometimes cheerful, outgoing, and radiant; at other times we're pensive or introverted.

At any time, we can ask: "Where does the chemistry feel best?" Identify that stage. Rehearse that healing chemistry. Then introduce that role into other parts of your dramatic life. Learn to make a real scene when you play the part of your choice.

There's no harm in shifting roles as long as we choose to shift. Much of the time, however, the shifts in our roles happen by accident.

Let's say I interview for 10 jobs and get no offers. Faced with this situation I could easily fall into a victim role with lines such as, "It doesn't matter what I say or do; I'll never get hired."

On the other hand, I could choose a victor's role by asking empowering questions, like "How can I view this experience as feedback instead of failure?" "What can I say or do differently the next time I interview." "Should I adjust my approach and go for a different kind of position?" "Could this be a chance to start my own business and turn my former employer into my first client?" Answering these questions is going to script me for a role with a much different line of action.

ACT NOW!

Too often I see negative scripting in my patients and in our society as a whole. Some people even script the chemistry of illness or injury for monetary gain. Easy litigation and greed make their super-objective an overly generous settlement from a workers' compensation or medical malpractice claim. Unfortunately, the longer they play the role of illness, the more real it becomes—truly a self-fulfilling prophecy. And even if their curtain falls on a huge settlement, these "victims" can end up with the chemistry of chronic illness.

Sometimes a friend or family member asks me, "Dale, are you always onstage?" I always answer, "You bet, and so is the rest of humanity. Our lives are a series of roles, and sometimes those scripts fail to serve us well. But any script can be changed, bit by bit. And since I am always trying to improve my health chemistry—to develop a new and better me—I try to stay in the healthiest act I can at all times. Only the people who are on stage all the time are for real. People who are on stage only when they are onstage are not for real!"

Ask yourself if you'd rather work with a grump who is real and is always playing the role of a doomsayer or with a grump who is act-ing happy. Which of these two people has the most potential for changing their own and your feeling chemistry for the better?

The real magic starts when our audience affirms our role and starts treating us like the character we want to be. When you play a role well enough to convince others, then you're managing your states with real skill. You've become a star in the Theater of Health.

7. *Acting is not a panacea.*

I see the discoveries of psychoneuroimmunology and the techniques of acting as a complement to good medical care—not as a substitute for such care. If you catch a severe cold or develop pneumonia, I would not simply advise you to act like a person with clear lungs and sinuses. I would tell you to drink plenty of clear fluids, stay warm, take an antibiotic if appropriate, and go to bed.

Likewise, if someone has traumatic injury from a car accident, I would not stand by that person's side and advise him to apply the Method and act like a pain-free person. Acting is not enough to stop bleeding or repair broken bones.

Acting techniques and strategies for releasing the pharmacy within are not exclusive strategies for health. I offer these acting strategies as additions and not replacements for more mainstream kinds of treatment.

Now, in some cases complementary alternative medical treatments can be the difference that makes the difference. If one of my patients develops breast cancer, I hope that she'll take advantage of the best that modern surgery, chemotherapy, and radiation can offer. In addition, I'll suggest that she use acting techniques to manage stress, moderate her emotional states, and script herself for the role of a long-term cancer survivor.

If this role becomes a reality, she might attribute her success to the alternative treatments. I'd be a little more cautious and say that it was the combination of all these strategies that made for her recovery. Acting techniques and the pursuit of healthy pleasures may be the extra elements that take her to the winner's circle.

I do not want people to believe that they can just act their way out of life-threatening illness or laugh themselves past an injury. We've heard that laughter is the best medicine. However, we also hear of people who die laughing, and may be true if laughter is the only medicine they depend on!

In short, acting well is not a complete script for health. Yet acting might dispense that extra dosage from the pharmacy within—from that personal pharmacy for which each individual has their own unique access code. The resulting chemistry may be that all-important something extra that augments the medical care already available—that something extra that tips the scale in our favor.

SCENE FOUR

....

STAGE

For each of us, life is a series of roles played out on various stages. One way to recreate your role is to take a fresh look at the various stages you occupy.

Observe your home, your office, and other key arenas in your life. Are these stages designed to enhance your maximum performance? If not, you can give your stages a makeover by choosing new lighting, props, scenery, colors, and even aromas.

Set your stage

The concept of staging gets us to the heart of *Act Now*—changing our feeling chemistry to promote health.

People in real estate know about the connection between chemistry and staging. Indeed, their profession calls upon them to set the stage of a home in a way that attracts buyers.

Barb Schwarz, an expert in educating real estate agents, conducts seminars on "Stage and Staging®" as they pertain to real estate. She wants prospective customers to walk into a living room and say, almost without thinking, "Oh, the chemistry of this place is great. This place feels *feels* like home already. Where do we sign the papers?"*

Many buildings are designed to trigger changes in our emotional state. Notable among them are places of worship. For Christians, a prominent example is the cathedral at Chartres in France. The architects of this magnificent structure designed a sanctuary that lifts the eyes and the spirit upward.

Standing in this great cathedral with its high ceiling and stained glass windows, you can almost sense a transcendent force entering your body from above. Here, the "faith-full" Christian senses a moving feeling and divine inner chemistry. Indeed, we often choose our usual place of worship because when we're there the chemistry is right.

Something like this happens to us in daily life also. Notice how your emotional state changes when you enter different environments— different "stages." For example, compare the feelings aroused in you when you enter an alley full of garbage, a cabin next to a serene lake, a crowded living room, or a smoky bar. The emotional flavors of various stages can affect us in ways that we seldom notice.

People recovering from alcohol, nicotine, or other drug addiction know about the power of staging, too. These people are commonly advised to design the environments of their homes and offices in a way that eliminates any triggers to use chemicals.

Many addicts, for example, listen to certain music, burn a certain brand of incense, sit in a certain chair, associate with a certain person, consume a particular food or beverage, or watch certain movies when getting high. For these people, recovering from addic-

---

* "Stage and Staging" as used in real estate is a federally registered trademark owned by Barb Schwarz.

tion means ridding their stages of these familiar sights, sounds, and smells and replacing them with healthful substitutes.

Staging also affects productivity. Perhaps you've worked in a crowded, dark, or dingy office. Given that kind of staging, I doubt that you looked forward to going to work, or that you felt much like doing your best work once you arrived there. People who have fun at work often point to the chemistry of pleasant physical surroundings as a welcome fringe benefit. Chances are, too, that these people are more productive and take fewer sick days.

Managers and supervisors are wise to consider the staging of their worksites. They might simply walk through the offices and halls of their companies and ask, "Would I like working in an environment like this?" Their answers set the stage for endorphin-raising changes in the work environment—changes that could impact not only the happiness and health of the staff but also the wealth of the company. Companies that recognize the importance of staging the work site often improve their bottom line as well.

Choose your props

Your stages in life are filled with props, whether you realize it or not. These may include your favorite plant, sofa, painting, or desk. Consider how different you'd feel about your home if you walked onto this familiar stage and suddenly discovered that these props were missing.

Many of us find certain stages so comforting that they become nests. We speak of a "nesting instinct" and of relaxing at home as "nesting." Dogs, cats, and other animals adopt certain places as nests, and so do human beings. That's exactly what happens when we get sick and decide to stay home from work or school for some

ACT NOW!

tender loving care. Hot tea and warm soup help, but the comfort we derive from lingering in a familiar space can play a role in our healing, too.

If the chemistry of your favorite nest or cozy nook helps you feel good, take some time to understand this fact. Consider how staging promotes this feeling and try to duplicate that staging whenever possible, provided it does no harm to yourself or others. If you travel often, I suggest that you take some part of your nest with you on the road for a dose of back home chemistry.

Research indicates that staging can influence recovery from surgery. One study compared surgical patients who stayed in a hospital room with a view of a park to those whose room faced a brick wall. On average, those with a view of the park left the hospital significantly sooner. Norman Cousins' decision to abandon his hospital room for a hotel suite might have played a role in his recovery from ankylosing spondylitis. (I mention Cousins' story in scene 1.) Certainly the founders of the hospice movement knew about the power of staging. They recognized that playing out our final act in a hospital is much different than performing the same scenes at home.

Some props have symbolic power. We use many props in medicine, such as stethoscopes, surgical instruments, magnetic resonance imagers, and more. In his book *Health and Healing*, Andrew Weil writes about the power of one venerable medical prop—the X-ray machine—to produce a placebo response:

> One doctor told me he had once treated a man in his late fifties who had lived for years with cutaneous warts over most of his body. The standard methods of removing them had only increased their numbers. Finally, on a whim, the doctor told the patient he would try out a new, experimental form of radiation that was somewhat risky but so powerful that it

Stage

might knock out the problem. He and a radiologist colleague had the man remove his clothes and stand in a darkened X-ray room. Then they made the machine hum loudly without actually emitting any X-rays. The next day, all of the warts fell off. They did not grow back.

The use of power props goes back centuries. Shamans bestow mystical power on common objects such as rocks, beads, pipes, and sticks. Priests, ministers, rabbis, and other religious leaders use candles, cups, chalices, and water to inspire feelings of devotion.

According to mythologist Joseph Campbell, medicine, religion, and acting most likely sprang from the same ancient roots. After all, the stages of our modern theaters bear a marked resemblance to the altars and pulpits we see in churches. Campbell adds that modern day examining rooms and surgical tables recall the religious stages and altars of ancient civilizations. These comparisons are of particular interest to me.

Perhaps this book will serve as a catalyst to bringing the fields of drama, religion and medicine in contact again. As a physician I'm proud of the monumental advances medical science has made. Perhaps we can advance even further by rekindling medicine's ancient kinship with the theater.

The practical suggestion behind this whole discussion is to set our stages and choose our props with care. If you want to set a new stage at work, for example, then fill your office with comforting and supportive props. A picture of your spouse, a drawing by a child, a favorite painting, or a wall hanging adorned with one of your favorite quotations can make all the difference. When you pack for a trip, take a cue from young children. Often they take along some object that triggers good feelings, such as a teddy bear, blanket, toy, or good luck charm. It works for them. Perhaps we should pamper

. . . .

ourselves with some childlike feeling chemistry while we're on the road, too.

Cleanliness is important, too. I don't know about you, but it's hard for me to settle into a stage that's cluttered or dirty. There's a good book titled *Clutter's Last Stand* that offers many suggestions for paring down possessions, getting organized, and otherwise setting more serene stages in our lives. These suggestions apply across many disciplines. Good editors know that half of their job is done when they go through a rough manuscript and cut all the unnecessary words. We can apply the same principle to setting the stages of our lives: Often less is more.

At the same time, remember that for some people, more can be more. This is particularly true for collectors. We have evidence that people who collect things as a hobby are always intellectually searching and thus are more alert. Because they compete to build up a prop warehouse, they have a goal. Moreover, their quest connects them to others, a cast of people with the same interest. Collectors are also challenged by the "hunt" and the reward of a find. For many collectors this is a happy pursuit that keeps a healing chemistry alive.

Face the music

As I was working on this book, I sometimes felt frustrated. I wanted to find a way to lift myself off the printed page and sit with you face-to-face. In this chapter, particularly, I'd like to be able to enter your home. If I could, I'd turn on beautiful, happy music as the background to your reading. Since I can't do this, I suggest that if at all possible, you turn on the most positive, uplifting music you can find and listen to it as you continue reading.

. . . .

Think for a moment what life would be like without music: no singing your favorite tunes; talk-only radio stations; no concerts; celebrations without songs like "Happy Birthday" or "I Love You Truly." To most of us, life without music is unthinkable.

Music can promote health and serenity. This is something that human beings have known for centuries. According to Robert Ornstein and David Sobel, the oldest known medical document is a papyrus referring to incantations used in healing the sick. And 2,500 years ago, the philosopher Pythagoras maintained that singing and playing an instrument every day could purge negative emotions such as worry, sorrow, and fear.

Throughout history, the rhythm and tempo of music have been used by healers to alter their own feelings and those of others. Music is still effectively used to tune up and turn on the chemistry of health.

To the ancient Greeks, Apollo was the god of both medicine and music. Greek myths also recount the legend of Orpheus, who used music to charm living creatures. These stories tell us Orpheus played such lovely music on his lyre that animals, trees, and stones followed him. Even rivers stopped flowing in the wake of his music.

Today we know such accounts are not literally true, yet modern science indicates that these myths may point to a core of truth. Dorothy Retallack, a researcher in California, studied the effects of music on the life of plants. She put a variety of plants in chambers with carefully controlled temperature and humidity, then piped in various kinds of music.

Judged by their angle of growth and the abundance of their flowers, the plants showed a special fondness for Bach and other baroque composers. Some of them, in fact, reached out almost as if to embrace the music, turning toward the speakers at 60-degree angles.

Recently I have seen evidence of the amazing results produced by playing carefully selected sounds to commercial crops of tomatoes, sunflowers, and orange trees. After exposure to these sounds, crop harvest was significantly improved and plants were noticeably healthier. If sound so remarkably changes the chemistry of these plants, then is it possible for human chemistry to be positively altered by music? It doesn't take a rocket scientist mentality to answer that question affirmatively. But it will take time, statistics, and careful science to confirm this intuition.

Dr. Georgi Lazanov, a Bulgarian psychiatrist, used music as part of a rapid learning program he helped develop in the mid-1960s. While listening to classical music, his students did relaxation exercises, closed their eyes, and listened to an instructor recite French phrases and translations in different voice intonations and rhythms. After the initial session, the students took a test to see how much they'd learned. The class average was 97 percent, meaning that most of the students learned 1,000 words that day—about half the working vocabulary of a language.

What's more, Dr. Lazanov's students experienced benefits that no one anticipated. Not only did their learning become more rapid and efficient, many reported they felt more relaxed and centered. Tensions, stress, headaches, and other pains seemed to decrease or disappear. Their physiological measurements seemed to back up these reports. It was common for students to experience lower blood pressure and muscle tension, as well as a slower pulse and breathing rhythm.

After that first experiment, organizations across the world began researching and applying Dr. Lazanov's methods under names like "accelerated learning" and "superlearning." As these researchers discovered, our bodies respond to music's rhythms. Music with 60 to 80 beats per minute (bpm), typical of baroque music, often produces a calming effect on our bodies. Music faster than 80 bpm can create an energizing effect. Much of country-western music—and this may be more than coincidence—is played at this faster tempo.

Baroque composers typically kept certain numbers and patterns in mind when they chose the beat, tempo, and harmony for their music. According to some reports, musicians in this period believed that particular sounds and rhythms could put human minds and bodies in tune, producing healing, calming effects.

Likewise, those who compare shamanistic healers from different cultures often marvel at the common features of shamanic music. I wonder if this commonality comes from the basic physiology of the human body, including the rhythm of the heartbeat and breathing. Some studies indicate that carefully selected music can enhance learning, memory, and concentration; reduce chronic pain by releasing endorphins; increase creativity; and alleviate stress.

Research also indicates that our heart rate synchronizes with music, speeding up or slowing down to match the tempo. Studies on the physiological effects of music also note that music affects respiratory rate, blood pressure, stomach contractions, hormone secretion, and the brain's electrical patterns.

This knowledge leads to many practical applications:

- Music played for people before, during, and after surgery can diminish anxiety and pain, reduce the need for medication, and speed recovery.

- Dentists acknowledge the therapeutic effects of music when they allow people to listen to tapes or the radio during drilling and tooth extractions.

- It is increasingly common to play music for women during childbirth. The theory is that music reduces pain and may decrease the length of labor.

· ·

- Music therapy is a widely accepted field, used as part of programs to treat cancer, respiratory problems, stroke, arthritis, and diabetes. Some music therapists have also reported success in working with autistic children.

- Music is standard fare in most aerobics classes. Exercise instructors and personal trainers know that music lifts moods and helps regulate breathing. Moving to rhythm can help us stretch muscles smoothly and gradually increase endurance.

Research in this area actively continues. There's even a new science—*cymatics*—devoted to studying the effects of different sounds and music on matter. In some of these studies, for example, researchers play sounds through solenoids (a type of magnet), and watch the patterns formed by metal filings near the solenoids. At certain sounds, filings assume geometrical shapes. It seems that even nonconscious matter can be patterned by the power of music.

Savor smells

A rich tradition of folk wisdom attests to the power of aromas in setting the stages of our lives. Indeed, aromas make up some of the most basic bonds between living things. Animals depend on scents to locate other members of their families. People who are in love savor the scent of their partner. And many of us find the smell of our food plays as big a role in our eating satisfaction as the taste of it. Anybody who's salivated after wandering past a candy shop knows this from experience.

The connection between aromas and emotions has a basis in physiology. The area of the brain involved in sensing and interpreting aromas is the limbic system. In terms of human evolution, this is

· ·

one of the oldest parts of the brain, and most of the human emotional response is also seated here.

The power of aroma is not lost on writers, directors, and other people who set real or imaginary stages for a living. In his great novel *Remembrance of Things Past*, Marcel Proust writes about the power of a single aroma to trigger vivid memories. Perhaps you, too, find that certain smells, such as the scent of a high school yearbook or the aroma of a favorite childhood meal, can release a flood of pleasant memories and positive feelings.

Actors sometimes use the same principle to prepare themselves for a role: They fill their dressing rooms with aromas that trigger the emotions they want to experience on stage. Such aroma kits may contain fragrances a particular actor links to happiness, romance, peace, satisfaction, sadness, fear, anger, embarrassment, remorse, and a host of other emotions. Those who have a "nose" for getting into a certain role learn to "sniff out the part" and trigger the appropriate chemistry. I hope that all of us can become nosy and learn to identify our happy-healthy smells.

Again, people in real estate come to mind. It's no accident when they urge home sellers to bake bread or make applesauce to create a "dramatic feeling" for a home showing. These professionals know the power of aromas to influence our feelings on a subliminal level. Surprisingly enough, there seem to be regional variations in the preferred aromas for home sales. In my home state of Minnesota, pine is a preferred scent. But in Georgia and other parts of the South, people tend to prefer the smell of peaches.

Certain aromas seem inherently happy—popcorn, chocolate, and cinnamon, for example. The chocolate smell is particularly interesting. Those of us who fear gaining weight know its perils. Yet there's some evidence that smelling chocolate can reduce the appetite. This may be due to a rise in endorphin levels associated with the scent of chocolate. (Besides inducing pleasure, endorphins can suppress appetite.) Studies of this phenomenon are taking place at the University of Chicago Taste and Smell Institute.

So, the next time you feel like reaching for a candy bar, take a good whiff of it instead and put the bar back on the shelf. If you can resist the temptation to actually eat the chocolate for a few minutes, your limbic system may be satisfied through the sense of smell alone.

If this experiment seems too dangerous, then just substitute another one of your favorite aromas and see what happens to your urge to snack. Perhaps you'd enjoy a low-calorie aroma like banana or strawberry.

Also, remember that individuals differ in their response to the same aroma. For me, it's not the scent of those expensive aftershave lotions at the big department stores that triggers the chemistry of happiness. Instead, I thrive on the aftershave lotion I wore as a junior in high school for the big date on Saturday night. Perhaps for you, too, this was a time in life when you owned the world and when men who wore Aqua Velva were invincible. That's why I still splash on Aqua Velva for any important presentation.

So, it pays to observe your own responses to aromas and to arrange your environment with these responses in mind. For you there may be an aroma of love and an aroma of anger, an aroma of elation and an aroma of sadness.

With a little thought and preparation, you can do some aroma therapy for yourself. Set your stage with aromas that promote relaxation and other healthy pleasures. These good feelings may yield chemistry that promotes your health and happiness.

Colors can elate, depress, and calm

Like aromas, colors can express the whole palette of human emotion. There are colors that seem to elate us and others that seem to depress us; there are colors that provoke anger and colors that calm us; perhaps there are even colors that enhance appetite and others that suppress it.

We dress in ways that both reflect and influence the way we feel. For instance, people wear darker colors to funerals and other somber occasions. Widows in some South American and Southern European countries wear black for a year after the death of their husbands to stay in the state of mourning. In contrast, people in other cultures who wish for an emotional lift may turn to brighter wardrobes for solace from grief or mourning.

Costumers are aware of this strategy and consciously choose colors to fit the characters. The next time you watch a movie or a play, see if you can draw any connection between the emotions that characters project and the colors of their costumes. The costumer for any show considers the current fashion for the part along with the emotional color of each role.

What are the colors of happiness? Each of us will answer that question differently. The colors you choose depend on your childhood experiences, your nationality, your skin color, and a host of other factors. I often classify color preferences by season. For example, there are people who prefer the rich, dark greens of mid summer grass and still others who are partial to the earth tones of fall. Whatever color you choose, people are bound to notice. They'll make comments such as "You look good in yellow" or "I bet you feel good in that color." And remember, when you feel good and look good, the right chemistry is on.

People connect through colors. Millions of Americans feel a common bond when they see the bold red, white, and blue of our flag. (By the way, these colors are common in the flags of many countries, as are yellow and green.) Other colors bind people together in religious rituals. Think, for instance, about the significance of purple to Christians, who remember this as the color of Jesus' robe on the day of his crucifixion.

Before leaving this subject of color, I'll note some fascinating studies on a certain shade of pink—Baker-Miller pink, to be precise. This particular hue is used in some prisons and psychiatric institutions with the aim of moderating emotions. The studies on Baker-Miller pink are not definitive, yet I for one would find it hard to remain angry for long if I spent most of my time in rooms painted this color. Perhaps further research in this area will yield pink police stations or mauve prisons!

This whole area of emotional response to color is something that those of us interested in complementary medicine need to learn more about. In this respect, the ancient Chinese and Ayurvedic healers may have been more advanced than we.

Let there be light!

Almost any theater technician can tell you about the power of lighting to affect an audience's moods. Lighting directors work with the hues, depth, and brightness of colors that will trigger the desired chemistry for both the cast and the audience.

There are many properties of light we must take into account: intensity, hue, color, contrast, and more. Our emotional responses may even differ with the type of light source. On a warm summer day, you might crave to eat lunch outside so that you can get a healthy dose of sunlight—especially if you work under fluorescent lights, which can cast a greenish hue on the people and objects in your office.

Lighting is important to people with seasonal affective disorder (SAD), a type of depression that seems to worsen for some people during dark, cloudy weather, and especially during the winter. Treatment for this condition commonly includes exposure to lamps that emit full-spectrum lighting, which is similar to sunlight.

In some cases, lighting directly influences the way people relate to each other. We tend to "come out" of ourselves and connect with people in brighter lighting. Darker lighting, on the other hand, increases our sense of privacy.

As a speaker, I know that it pays to turn the lights in a room up as high as they'll go when I want members of my audience to laugh and talk to each other a lot. This may not be true for comedians who tell risque jokes, who often work in dimly lit nightclubs. Many in the audience would not be comfortable being seen as they laugh at off-color entertainment, so the lights are dimmed to preserve a sense of anonymity. In darkness, people often feel more private and laugh with less embarrassment.

While we're in dim lighting, our sense of hearing may even be diminished. On a dimly lit stage, actors commonly speak louder to be heard by the audience. As a professional speaker, I realize that my message will be heard better when the lights are up.

However, dim lighting is also our preference for resting, relaxing, and intimate touching. During such activities, few of us wish to be caught in the spotlight.

Once you grasp the power of lighting, color, music, aromas, and other aspects of staging to influence your feelings, you may never again gloss over these aspects of your environment. Considering the profound way that these factors affect our feelings, we can use them to enhance a chemistry of happiness and health.

All the world's a stage. So set your stage for health, wealth, and happiness.

SCENE FIVE

....

COSTUME

Stanislavski placed great emphasis on costuming when working with acting students. In fact, he sometimes said that the moment of putting on a costume was a pivotal one in an actor's preparation for a role. Stanislavski understood that changing our external appearance has the power to change our internal chemistry as well. Costumes are living, moving scenery, and we'll do well to costume ourselves with immaculate attention. The idea is to costume ourselves appropriately for roles of happiness and health.

For me, costuming is a broad term that includes clothing, cosmetics, accessories, hairstyle, facial expression, and even posture. In this chapter I'll touch on all these topics.

Put on a new face

Some people say that you can't change your face. I beg to differ. I choose to agree with my grandmother, who often said to someone with a sad expression, "Honey, you'd better change your face before it hardens that way."

· ·

When I speak about acting and health, I devote much time to strategies for changing this essential part of our costume. Besides, I'm fond of word plays, and the subject of facial expression is pregnant with puns. For example, I urge my audiences not to worry about saving face, and I talk unashamedly about increasing your face value by putting your best face forward. Face it! A smile promotes the chemistry of happiness and helps everyone feel better.

Actors also know about the dramatic power of makeup. They must put on the mask that gets them into the desired chemistry for the personality of their role. It is of interest to word lovers that the word personality is derived from the Latin word *persona* which means a mask.

Cosmetic companies focus on helping to create images of facial and body happiness. The judicious use of makeup can add color to life in more ways than one. Lately I've been telling other health care providers that cosmetologists may be our colleagues in healing.

Dressing up, applying makeup, costuming with jewelry—all these simple acts can alter self-concept and, along with it, the chemistry of feeling. Nurses at retirement homes, hospitals, and hospices tell me what happens to women residents when the beautician comes to visit. Not only do these residents look better, they become more active, communicative, and sociable after they've been "fixed up." Friends and relatives often will tell them how nice you look and they will respond, "And how good I feel." Moreover, these women may keep up the positive act for several days. Sometimes it's the people undergoing chemotherapy or other intensive treatments who most value being "done up."

Hair color is another significant factor. I have a relative who is 90 years young, and I've never seen her in anything but red hair. For years this bothered me, and I kiddingly suggested to other members of the family that she was just putting on an act. Today, as I

· ·

learn more about the relationship between acting and health, my attitudes are changing. I'm beginning to think that her vigor may be partly due to the role she's played for so long—a role in which hair coloring and acting youthful are crucial.

By far, my favorite technique for re-costuming the face is smiling. I like to say that your day goes the way the corners of your mouth go. When the corners of your mouth are up, you're up also. (When you're down in the mouth—well, you get the point.) It's more important what you wear from ear to ear than what you wear from head to toe. By costuming your face in this way, you get more "smileage" out of life.

One of the things that most of us want to see in any photograph of ourselves is a smile on our face. Professional photographers know this, which is why they insist on making you say silly things like "cheers," "cheese," "money," or other words that automatically put your lips and face into the smile position. Likewise, the last grooming task I perform—after shaving, washing my face, combing my hair, and brushing my teeth—is to take a last look in the mirror and smile at myself. I want to alter my feeling chemistry before I launch out into the world to meet other people.

I bet you do the same. Be honest now. How often before that important meeting, interview, or date have you looked into the mirror and given yourself a big smile or grin? I hope you do so often, because a smile is one of the easiest and most dramatic techniques for triggering the chemistry of good feeling.

Behind the outwardly simple act of smiling is some complex physiology. This configuration of the face subtly alters your biochemistry, sending a message to the mind-body that says, "Hey, you, send in the clowns!"

Just put a smile on your face. Do it right now. Feels good, doesn't it? I believe you can almost sense those endorphins being released when you smile.

I know people who get up in the morning, go to the window, look out to check the weather, and groan, "Good God—morning." Other people look out and say the same three words in a different way: "Good morning, God." The second group of people usually begin the day with a smile on their faces. They make their own weather. This self-made weather becomes the climate of their existence and a significant factor in the emotional environment—not only in their lives but in the lives of those about them.

We all know that smiling reflects happy feelings. Yet most of us forget that we can induce new thoughts and feelings by the mere act of smiling. In other words, we smile when we feel happy, but we also feel happy when we smile.

We can smile at any time. We don't have to wait until we *feel* joyful or optimistic before we smile. In fact, smiling may usher in those very feelings of joy and optimism. I sometimes ask the people in my audiences to frown and then write down the first thought that comes to mind. For most people, that thought is a neutral or negative thought. But ask them to smile and that first thought usually changes to a positive, affirming, optimistic one.

There's a simple game I use with audiences to demonstrate the power of facial expression to alter emotions. I begin by giving each person two pages of cartoons, with four cartoons on each page. Then I ask everyone to rate, on a scale of 1 to 10, how funny each cartoon is.

The catch is I require them to write down their ratings in a rather unusual way: They must hold the pen in their mouths! Furthermore, when rating the first page of cartoons, they must hold the pen only with their lips. And when rating the second page, they must hold the pen only with their teeth. Then they add the total of the four scores for each page.

The results I get are fairly consistent: Usually about 20 percent of the audience finds the first page of cartoons funnier, while 80 to 90 percent rate the second page as funnier.

What my audiences don't know is that the same eight cartoons are randomly distributed in 16 different ways on the two pages. I believe that the differences in ratings for the two pages are probably not due to the cartoons themselves but to people's facial expressions while rating them. Holding a pen with their lips forces their faces into a frown while rating the first page, and holding the pen with their teeth while rating the second page induces a smile. The humor these people find in the cartoons may have more to do with their mouths than with what they see on a page.

Grin and share it

Smiles are contagious. Every time you smile, you send a nonverbal message that registers with the people who see you. Smiling is a great way to create a connecting chemistry. A smile is a gift we give to and receive from others. This is much the same as wrapping a gift in high-quality wrapping paper or putting an attractive frame on a picture. People tend to perceive your "packaging" as being more valuable when it's "wrapped up" in a pleasant look.

There's some evidence that people who smile frequently enjoy better family relationships; relate more effectively with clients, customers, and supervisors; get more tips; and win more promotions. Besides triggering the chemistry of health, smiling may deliver more wealth to you as well. Department store clerks who smile often make more in commissions, and I've been told that blackjack

ACT NOW!

dealers in Las Vegas who smile consistently take in 5 percent more for the house. Let's sum it up by saying that smiling is a free way to increase your face value—an investment that pays handsome dividends.

Dress "up"

"Rent or buy one of our costumes. Put it on . . . and become someone else!"

Several years ago, I saw this headline shortly before Halloween on a billboard outside a costume store. How true, I thought. If only I could persuade more of my patients to change their costuming, they could feel so much better.

One hallmark of depressed people is a neglect of basic hygiene and grooming. Often these people are lax about getting dressed, combing and washing their hair, shaving, and so on. I would say that these people *stop costuming*. One of the ways to help counter depression, then, is to give time and meticulous attention to costuming.

Clothing is a key part of costuming. The clothes we wear signal the role in life we choose to play. There are the "power suits" and other costumes worn by people in business who wish to dress for success. There are the costumes of rebels, nonconformists, and others who want to send the message, "I don't go along with the crowd." And there are the more casual costumes we adopt during weekends and vacations. I'm sure you can think of more examples.

My suggestion is that you choose your costume in a way that projects the emotions—the chemistry—you want to experience. And if you make this chemistry consistently, it becomes a habit—the real you. I think this idea is especially important for older people.

Costume

Those of us age 60 and over need to costume with care. Just because you're 65, 75, or 85 doesn't mean you have to dress your age. In fact, people who are 90 may be far better off if they dressed as if they were 50 or 60. I tell the "VPs" (vintage people) in my audiences to throw out their polyester slacks and leisure suits and stay fashionable. As for myself, I often try to dress like successful business people in their 40s. I know that if I dress like the 70–year–old retiree who scripts himself to act old, then I, too, can catch that old feeling. But if I can break out of the stereotypical role for old age, I can have a renewed, healthier, and happier chemistry.

I would also recommend that you go for the labels. If it's within your budget, pay up and go for quality that you can see. It used to upset me that some people attach so much importance to wearing shirts with a fancy insignia or other trendy labels. Now I say, If the presence of a label changes the way you feel about yourself, then more power to the label and to you. You're putting on a good act.

I often think about this when selecting a suit to wear for a meeting or speech. In my closet is a blue suit I bought on sale for $200. Despite its modest price, this suit fits me well and even looks decent. Nonetheless, I usually opt for another blue suit, one I bought for $700. Now, I doubt that many people notice any difference in appearance between these two suits. Even I have a hard time telling the difference sometimes. Yet I feel more classy in the $700 suit, so I usually suit up.

Accessories such as jewelry and scarves have a special way of helping some people doll up. Others have certain items of clothing that make them feel special. If what you wear is within the bounds of good taste and promotes a feel-good chemistry on your part, then keep it up.

The point is that logic need not always be the final criterion in choosing our costumes. For me, for many years it was logical to find clothing in the bargain basements. And sometimes the quality was as good there as in the expensive fashion stores. But as we are often told, you usually get what you pay for. So if what looks and feels right for you is important, if the expensive designer clothes make you feel better about yourself, then follow your feelings. Dress "up."

It's all done with mirrors

Recently I read a study about the behavior of people who sell products over the phone. One telemarketing company had a policy of positioning its sales representatives in front of mirrors. Soon afterward the company's profits began going up. Sales representatives who viewed themselves in a mirror while making calls sold 17 percent more than those without mirrors. Mirrors helped the salespeople "reflect" on the impression their expression made on customers.

My hunch is that this increase resulted in part from more frequent smiling. Notice what happens when people see themselves in a mirror. More often than not, they smile. When you talk to effective salespeople over the phone, you can almost hear them smile.

This observation leads to a practical strategy: When costuming for the day, stand in front of a mirror. Also, install mirrors around your house, your office, and other stages in your life. Use mirrors as reminders to put on the costume of happiness, and remember that the best piece of costume jewelry is the sight of your teeth sparkling in a big smile.

The power of posture

Judy, age 52, is a very competent, hard-driving office manager. Like many people, she had a consuming fear that her nagging back pain was a serious problem that would get progressively worse. Judy saw herself confined to a wheelchair and adopting the stereotyped little old lady (LOL) position—hunched forward with drooping shoulders and a rounded back. This image depressed her. And because she felt depressed, she assumed the body language of depression: slumped shoulders with trunk slouching forward. This, in turn, increased her odds of becoming precisely what she feared.

Several of Judy's friends observed her characteristic posture and asked if she felt depressed. I suspect it was the other way around: Judy adopted a depressed posture, so then she felt depressed. Her negative body language made it easier for her to think negative thoughts and feel negative feelings. And when her friends started to see her as depressed, this only compounded her negative chemistry. Our chemistry depends not only how we act but upon how others react to us.

At the time I saw Judy, I was just beginning to understand what Stanislavski taught—that if you lead with the body, the mind will follow. His idea was echoed by Frederik Alexander, an actor and founder of the Alexander technique. I often repeat to myself a short saying that sums up the essence of this technique: "Let my neck be free to let my head go forward and up, to let my back lengthen and widen."

The words up, out and widening sum up the Alexander technique and the role of posture in the act of health. If we are going to have outstanding health, we need to sit tall and stand up.

With Alexander's teachings in mind, I asked Judy to think of me as her acting coach. She was now in acting school, and we were going to costume her for several different parts. For each of the parts, I would ask her to assume an exaggerated body posture that would depict the character.

First I asked Judy to play a sad, despondent young woman. For this role, Judy sat slouched forward, head down, eyes downcast, corners of the mouth turned down, and shoulders rolled forward. In this position, her body was folding inward on itself. Even Judy's breathing seemed to turn inward in short, choppy, sob-like wheezes. Her thoughts, too, started to turn inward and she became self-centered. Because her body adopted a sad costume, her thoughts and speech patterns naturally developed along those negative lines.

I asked her what she was feeling and thinking: "How's the chemistry, Judy?" She almost broke into tears. How alone she felt, how out of touch, how apart from the world. She thought of unpleasant relationships and personal failures in her life. Masterfully she assumed the role of a worried, dejected, defeated, crestfallen person. Her emotional chemistry followed where her body led.

Next I assigned Judy a new role—that of a bubbly, vigorous, bouncy, successful woman of 55 who has just won the lottery and rekindled a romance with her high school sweetheart.

Judy immediately sat up straight, her shoulders back, her head and neck held proudly. Her ear and rear were in the perfect vertical alignment of erect posture. There was a twinkle in her eyes. A grin came to her face, and she even found herself laughing. Her hands and arms were held out. Her body appeared open, receptive, blossoming. Her breathing deepened and projected outward. She was filled with spark, fire, life.

"Oh, Judy. You're the perfect person for this part," I said. "What are you feeling? What are you thinking?"

You guessed it. She was experiencing wonderful, warm feelings of happiness and good health—thoughts of love, optimism, and hope. By repositioning her body, Judy had put on the body costume of happiness and created a new body image. That image was conveyed to her brain, and her brain responded with positive thoughts.

Test it yourself

Have you ever stood in front of the mirror, feeling glum and not liking what you see and the way you feel? The next time you do, smile at yourself. Then stand straighter, vertically aligning your ear and your rear. Next, monitor your thoughts and feelings. Experience for yourself how difficult it is to sustain negative attitudes when you assume this new body stance. Chances are this simple exercise will help you see a new you.

This is what Tom, another patient of mine, experienced. In high school, Tom was looked upon as the all-American boy. Now a middle-aged lawyer, he came into my office one day at the urging of his family. He looked substantially older than his 55 years. He sat stooped forward, with rounded lower back, humped upper back, forward-jutting chin, and rolled shoulders.

Tom looked at himself in the mirror one day and got the picture. He perceived that age was fast taking its toll. And, as often happens, his thoughts followed his body messages. Tom became convinced he was beginning to feel old as well as look old. The sight of his body posture started to convince him that his life was all downhill from here. Without realizing it, Tom had scripted himself into the role—into the chemistry—of an old man.

Tom wondered if he was getting osteoporosis. He'd seen a magazine advertisement with a photograph of a woman in the little old

ACT NOW!

lady pose. Splashed across the top was a headline that said "Osteoporosis can do this to you!" Readers were then urged to buy an expensive calcium supplement. The message was clear: Stooped posture is the result of calcium deficit. Meanwhile the older woman's statuesque young daughter, also present in the picture, said, "If only mother had known about ground up oyster shells from Tahiti, she wouldn't have her osteoporosis problem."

Nonsense. Older women and some men can have serious problems with osteoporosis, but more often the humped, bent-over look results not from osteoporosis but from a lifetime of poor posture. The woman Tom saw in the advertisement probably lost her spinal flexibility and shape because of poor sitting and sleeping posture habits. If she had maintained spinal flexibility and followed a practice such as the Alexander technique she would not only have better posture and look younger but would diminish the risk of developing osteoporosis.

It's a common story. Once many people leave high school, they start to lose their youthful mobility and flexibility, especially the ability to arch the back.

After leaving school, the older woman in the advertisement probably went to work sitting at a desk or bending over a table or counter. Later she may have married and bent forward to do household chores or lift babies from the crib. She probably slouched while holding the children or relaxing from housework. All these things contributed to poor posture.

At any rate, I told Tom not to worry about permanently settling into the little old man posture. While Tom appeared to be degenerating, he could in fact regenerate by putting on a new body costume and playing a new role. While on a new playing field—a new stage—he could still score big, much like he did as a youthful athlete. I knew he could regain much of the youthfulness of his back, not to mention the rest of his body and mind, if he would start a back-arching and stretching program and launch an all-out effort to change his posture habits.

What are some of those habits? I've already mentioned costuming in front of a mirror. Another is to preserve the curve in the small of your lower back. For many years, I told people to avoid this arch in the lower back (called the lumbar lordotic curve). Many of us in the medical community believed that sustaining this curve would result in future problems. You might say we were "arch enemies" of this posture. In fact, we encouraged people to flatten the lower back and avoid sleeping on their stomachs.

Today our advice has turned around 180 degrees. Now we're giving people arching exercises to help regenerate bad backs. I give most of my patients back-arching exercises and tell them it's okay to sleep on their stomachs if that feels comfortable. This is consistent with my general prescription to listen to Mother Nature, a wise director who wants us to access the chemistry of good health.

Finally, give some attention to your characteristic gestures. Notice what happens to your emotional state when you fold your posture inward and downward. Try it now: Slouch forward. Move your shoulders toward your chest. Close your eyes, frown, and take shallow breaths. This is a classic posture of introversion, repression, and depression.

Now reverse all the gestures you just made. Thrust your shoulders back and then raise your arms upward and outward, as if you're preparing to hug someone. Look up toward the ceiling or make eye contact with another person. Also take a long, slow, expanding deep breath. Now smile a broad smile—one that's big enough to show your teeth.

ACT NOW!

Congratulations. You just adopted a posture of happiness, optimism, caring, and connection with others. From here it's just a short step to shouting with joy or bursting with laughter.

You can do this exercise any time you're feeling depressed or lazy. I call it the "posture prescription." And if you find yourself in a place where it's not feasible to make such dramatic changes in posture, then just visualize yourself doing the exercise. Mentally costuming yourself with the posture of happiness may be enough to dilute negative feelings and clear a path for optimism and joy.

Stanislavski would say, "Actors must know how to put on and wear a costume and how to appropriately use proper body language and stage props. Only then can they feel themselves in the part and the part in themselves."

SCENE SIX

·····················

SCRIPT

Each day we live out scripts for roles that last a lifetime. By scripts, I mean the lines we speak. In essence, a script is a set of instructions for what to say while we're on the stage of daily life. These instructions, in turn, are based on our attitudes and beliefs.

Many people play out scripts based on unworkable beliefs—lines scripted long ago by others. And there are a legion of these "others"—parents, siblings, relatives, peers, teachers, and religious leaders, to name a few. Our scripts are also richly endowed with the legacy of our family and cultural philosophy, religion, literature, and science.

You can choose a new script

Our scripts have been written and rewritten for centuries by many playwrights. So none of us should hesitate to do some rewriting today. None of us has to accept shallow scripts. All the discoveries of modern cognitive psychology add up to one insight: You can choose to modify an old script at any point. You can speak new lines, create new actions, make new chemistry. You can redirect and even rename your play, and in the process you can become your own play-*right.*

We feel the way we script

Cognitive psychology is one of the fastest-growing and most effective types of mental health treatment available today. The word *cognitive* comes from *cognition*, which means *thinking*. And the key premise of cognitive psychology is that *we feel the way we think.* No external event causes us to feel a certain way. Rather, our feelings flow from how we think and what we say to ourselves about those events.

Earlier in this book I proposed that feelings are chemistry, and that the chemistry of feelings can be changed in two ways: by actions or by thought. In scripting, we emphasize the influence of thought. It becomes evident that we can "think up" our chemistry. Our thoughts can access our healing pharmacy within. For me, the scientific evidence for this phenomenon is one of the most exciting discoveries of my lifetime.

While the scientific support is new, the idea is ancient. "We are what we think," said the Buddha. "All that we are arises with our thoughts. With our thoughts, we make the world." The book of Proverbs in the Bible reminds us that, "As a man thinketh in his heart, so is he."

I can offer several examples. Say, for instance, that a hard working 50-year-old truck driver named Sam experiences a serious heart attack in a city far from home. He has just purchased a new rig, and his family's livelihood depends on his working even harder. Yet his physician says, "Sam, you must have a coronary bypass operation. And after that I advise you to consider changing jobs because you need to control your stress, diet, and exercise more wisely. You need to change your whole act."

Sam's reaction is one of concern, fear, and anger. Given these feelings, he could blame others for his plight and cry foul: "Trucking is all I know how to do. It's my whole life. I'm just beginning to make it, and now it's the end."

There is another option. Sam could do some rewriting. He could listen to the directors of his life script who are telling him that, with a change of lifestyle, he could regenerate much of his cardiovascular condition and expect to live a long and happy life. He could congratulate himself for taking out health and disability insurance, thus avoiding a total business setback. And he could see this situation as an opportunity to live out a script titled, "Do What You Love and the Chemistry Will Follow."

As another example, say a young professional in his first year out of college finds out he owes $2,000 more in income taxes than he expected. "How terrible!" he shrieks. "How could this happen? I don't deserve this."

That's one possible reaction. Yet he could have also said, "Wow! I owe more in taxes. I don't relish parting with the money, but this means that I made a lot more money last year than the year before. Next year I'll prepare for this by setting aside some extra money for tax payments. The way things are going, I can easily afford it."

I'm sure you see the difference between these scripts. What people often forget is that they can lead to different sets of feelings. With the first script, the young man feels angry, suspicious, and resentful. With the second, he can feel like a winner.

Notice that the initial event—the extra tax liability—is the same in both scripts. What, then, leads to the difference in the lines spoken? According to cognitive psychologists, it is a set of core beliefs. These

ACT NOW!

beliefs represent basic values and fundamental judgments about people and the world. In the first case, the man's script was based on core beliefs such as:

- I'm a victim of circumstances I cannot control.

- Losing money is the worst thing that could happen to me.

- Things should turn out exactly the way I expect them to. If they don't, it's terrible.

Contrast that list with the following beliefs that underlie the second script:

- The things that happen to me usually result from my own decisions and actions.

- Things will not always turn out the way I expect, and I can live with that.

- I can change my behavior based on the consequences I experience.

- Good things are in store for me in life.

When it comes to scripting, most of us can benefit from a little mental housecleaning. We can examine our scripts, looking for any core beliefs that are off-track. Then we can rewrite our scripts, basing our new lines on beliefs that promote positive feelings.

In short, we can respond to any event with either clause from the first line of Dickens' *Tale of Two Cities:* "It was the best of times, it was the worst of times." The clause we eventually choose depends less on the event than on our core beliefs.

In his moving book, *Man's Search for Meaning,* psychiatrist Viktor Frankl described his experiences as a survivor of Auschwitz, the Nazi death camp. Experiences as a prisoner, wrote Frankl, convinced him that "everything can be taken from a man but one thing: the last of human freedoms—to choose one's own attitude in any given set of circumstances, to choose one's own way." When it comes to rewriting beliefs, I take courage from Frankl's ability to choose his attitudes even in harsh, brutal conditions.

Examine your current script

The first step to changing your life script is to lay bare the part that you're currently playing. This means taking a close look at the lines you say, either to others or to yourself. The goal here is to search for core beliefs that no longer serve you.

Albert Ellis, one of the most influential cognitive psychologists, talks about three core beliefs (scripts) that are almost guaranteed to help us feel miserable:

- Other people should behave exactly the way I expect.

- I should always behave exactly the way I expect.

- Events should always turn out exactly the way I expect.

Plainly, these are unworkable beliefs. In the real world, I do not control other people's behavior. Sometimes they will act in ways that surprise me. Sometimes, too, I make mistakes, and this leads to consequences that I don't always expect or want. If I live by these three beliefs, I will constantly be at war with reality. What's more, I'll spend much of my life feeling sad, mad, or afraid. Evidence from psychoneuroimmunology suggests that these negative emotions can be linked to many illnesses.

The three basic beliefs that Ellis mentions have hundreds of variations. Some of them are listed on the next page. As you read the list, check off any lines that you've spoken or thought recently:

ACT NOW!

—*I'll never amount to anything.*

—*Other people have so much better luck than I do.*

—*I don't deserve to succeed.*

—*I always say stupid things when I meet new people.*

—*I will die at an early age because my parents did.*

—*Asking for help is a sign of weakness.*

—*I hate it when other people disagree with me.*

—*I have to be right all the time.*

—*I can succeed all the time if I try hard enough.*

—*I have to win all the time.*

—*Making a mistake is a disaster.*

—*If people knew me as I really am, they would hate me.*

—*If I fail, I'm a terrible person.*

—*People just can't be trusted.*

—*I should never feel sad.*

—*The world is not a safe place.*

—*Bad things come in threes.*

—*Good relationships don't last long.*

— *Most people are happier than I am.*

—*Romance is only for young people.*

—*If I get attached to other people, they'll just leave.*

—*Anyone I love will eventually abandon me.*

And of course, there are many more negative scripts.

If you checked any of the items on this list, you may be acting from a script that's producing an inner chemistry of depression, anxiety, or fear. Consider taking the next logical step and change the script.

Rewrite your script

As almost any creative playwright will tell you, there are many ways to revise —"re-right"—a script. Use the following suggestions to get started, and then do what works for you.

Look for judgmental words

Unworkable beliefs are usually absolute—that is, they don't allow any exceptions. The word *always* is a sure-fire signal of such absolute statements, as in, "Events should always turn out the way I want them to." Beliefs that include this word usually express an unrealistic judgment about the world.

Other words to look out for are these:

- *Should*—"People should always behave the way I want them to."

- *Have to*—"I have to do it this way. I've got no choice."

- *Can't*—"I can't do anything about this problem."

- *Either-or*—"Either do it my way or hit the highway."

When you encounter a line that includes any of these words, rewrite the line with more flexible, less judgmental words. See the examples on the next page.

ACT NOW!

Original line—People *should* always behave the way I want them to.

Revised line—I'd *prefer* that people behave the way I want them to, but I can live with it if they don't. (As Ellis often suggests, we can avoid "shoulding" on ourselves and others.)

Original line—I *have* to do it this way.

Revised line—I *usually* do it this way. Perhaps another way would work better.

I *choose* to do it this way.

Original line—I *can't* do anything about this situation.

Revised line—I *haven't* done anything about this situation yet, and it's time to start.

Original line—*Either* do it my way, *or* don't do it.

Revised line—I'd *prefer* that you do it this way. If you have another suggestion, let's talk.

Ask powerful questions

Our thinking is shaped by questions. Most of us have habitual questions—those that we ask ourselves over and over again. Few of us realize the power of these habitual questions to shape our thinking and, in turn, our actions.

Certain questions are more powerful than others. By that I mean that some questions naturally invite answers that allow for change, help us learn, and put us back in charge of our lives.

As an example, consider the medical transcription secretary who reports to work one Monday morning, only to discover that he's getting laid off. Faced with this situation, his mind immediately fills with questions: "Why does this always happen to me? What did I do to deserve this?" You can almost predict the answers: "I must be a failure. I must have made some terrible mistake that no one told me about."

These answers may be off base. Perhaps this person's layoff was part of a restructuring that affected hundreds of people. It's also possible that his job performance had nothing to do with getting laid off. Perhaps he was simply an excellent worker caught up in a round of budget cuts. He might have discovered these facts had he asked a different set of questions: "Is this layoff tied to my job performance?" "Is there anything I could have done to avoid this?" "Did anyone else get laid off?"

A valuable practice, then, is to monitor your questions. Search out questions that lead to stale roles, tired lines, and negative feelings. Replace these questions with ones that open up possibilities and invite new emotional responses. Such questions are:

- How can I use this experience to gain new skills?
- What am I willing to do to solve this problem?
- What do I enjoy about my life right now?
- Who loves me?
- Who do I love?
- How can I use my skills to contribute to others?

ACT NOW!

- What gifts have I received from others?

- What can I give back to others?

George Bernard Shaw knew the power of questions when he wrote, "Some men see things as they are, and say 'Why?' I dream of things that never were, and say, 'Why not?'"

Use the "magic if" to promote your imagination

Stanislavski referred to the "magic if" as a tool to stimulate the imagination of his students and lead to convincing action on stage. This technique involves posing a question to yourself that includes the word *if:* What *if* I found myself in this character's circumstances? What would I say and what would I think *if* this character's purpose in life was my purpose? What would I do next?

Stanislavski insisted that the magic *if* has the power to take actors into the hearts and minds of their characters. Any of us can use the same technique. For example, we can ask: What *if* I were living the life of my dreams? *If* that were true, then where would I live? How would I spend my time? Who would I routinely see? Where would I work? Asking these questions leads naturally to a through line of actions that can help us achieve our goals.

Here's another example: Ask yourself, "What *if* I were enjoying a consistent state of high-level health? *If* that were true, then what habits would I cultivate? What would I eat? How would I exercise? How would I handle stress?" If you have a chronic illness, ask, "How can I rethink my part and act in a way that optimally supports my current treatment?"

The magic if allows us to spontaneously generate many strategies for achieving health and good feelings. Use the magic if to inspire new lines and actions for the script of your choice.

Here Stanislavski would say:"When you act the 'magic if,' you will pass from the plane of actual reality into the plane of another life—a life that you have imagined and created for yourself. 'As if' acting is a lever that transports you into another world—a world where your chemistry is different!"

Start with small changes

As you revise your script, remember that you don't have to rewrite whole acts or scenes all at once. Instead, start by changing your script a few words or lines at a time. Sometimes the simplest changes are the most significant. Directors of a play may effect a profound change in feeling through a minor change in script or stage direction. We, too, are like these theater directors when it comes to enhancing healthy feelings.

One useful trick is to ask yourself another "if" question: "What if I could only make two changes in my script right now? What two or three basic changes in my lines or stage actions would launch me into the role of happiness and health?"

I urge everyone to begin with two stage directions: straighten your posture as described in scene 5, and smile. Just these two simple, basic actions will trigger a resulting script (thought) modification that has the potential for making positive changes in your feeling chemistry—and consequently in your health.

You may feel that you're faking it at first, but with practice these habits will become the real you. Eventually what feels wrong to you today will start to feel right. You will develop a comfortable new habit by creating a new act.

Avoid analyzing

When you lay bare the flaws in your current script, you might be tempted to ask: "Why was my script written like this? And who put these crazy lines in here in the first place?"

Often these questions have no certain answers. We can burn up hours, days, and even years of our lives analyzing ourselves and searching for something or someone to blame for lame lines and crazy stage directions. We could get so busy delving into our script's history that we never get around to actually changing the script.

I find another approach to be more useful. Sometimes we won't understand why a script is written the way it is or who the original playwright was. We can simply accept this fact and just get on with the business of scripting a new role. Instead of asking why or who, ask what and how. What do I want to do, have, and be during my lifetime? How can I achieve the things that are most important to me? What small alterations in my actions and lines can I make today that will fulfill my objectives? Asking these questions moves us into action and invites us to think in new ways.

Usually it is much more effective and enjoyable to write a script for positive feeling than it is to get involved with the gut wrenching exercise of trying to purge a script of negative feelings. If we think and act to develop a more positive chemistry, then the negative chemistry will be neutralized. If we accentuate the positive, we can eliminate the negative to a large degree. And approaching something pos"I"tively is surely more fun.

Script yourself young

As we age, none of us has to accept a script that includes stereotypes about aging. No matter how old we are, none of us has to act old. At any age, we can live out a script that keeps us young in mind and spirit. Observe how children seek out and dispense fun and laughter—unashamedly, without guilt. See how they wonder and revel in newness, ambiguity, disorder, change, and the beauty of nature.

I am not suggesting that "chronologically gifted" people act childish. What I am suggesting is that people act childlike. We can take time to gaze at a sunset, play games, ask questions, search out new experiences, learn a new language, keep up with current technology, become computer literate, and embrace change. Expect change, look for change, and welcome change as an opportunity to learn, grow, and cultivate active, youthful thinking. Emulate children.

And most of all, laugh. From age of two to four, children may laugh up to 400 times per day. This runs counter to the scripts of solemn and serious adults. We teach children not to laugh in school, not to laugh in church, and not to laugh at the supper table. We tell children to "stop monkeying around" and to "stop acting so silly." We also tell them to get serious and get to work.

Even though we say we value humor, we somehow convey the message to our children that laughter is a rare commodity that has little place in the world of adults. Too often this writes a script for children that robs them of some potent ways to change their feeling chemistry for the better.

My message for anyone who wants to feel younger is to start acting younger. Study what children say and do, then rewrite your script with their best ideas in mind.

Watch your language

Earlier in this chapter I mentioned some words that are tip-offs to unworkable core beliefs—*can't, should,* and others. After you get some experience with purging these initial words, take a look at your vocabulary in general. As you do, remember that the words we use to describe an experience influence how we feel about that experience.

Suppose my wife is an hour late coming home, which foils my plans for dinner. The next day I say to my neighbor, "She was late, and it was such a disaster." That last word is not the best or most accurate adjective that I could have chosen. Most of the time, after all, eating a late dinner is not really a disaster. Nobody dies. No one gets sick. No one loses money. At most, I lose an hour and get pretty hungry. Eating late might be a disappointment, but it's not a disaster. I could have said it this way instead: "She was late, and it was such an inconvenience." In terms of my emotional response, those two words mean a world of difference.

So, think again about that child who gets into everything. Perhaps he's just curious or inquisitive. And rethink the way you talk about that supervisor who is so picky. Perhaps she's just focused on details.

Another word to watch for is *but*. Each time you say this word, see if you can use the word *and* instead:

- "I want to go on a long walk *but* it's raining" becomes, "I want to go on a long walk *and* it's raining—so I'll take my umbrella."

- "I want to start building up my savings account *but* I only have $50 per month to spare" changes to, "I want to start building up my savings account *and* I have $50 per month to spare. I can start small for now, get into the habit of saving, and save more as I find more ways to cut my expenses."

- "I would like to exercise more *but* I can't find the time" becomes, "I would like to exercise more *and* I can start by walking an extra flight of stairs each day."

- "I'm becoming overweight *but* I can't diet" changes to, "I'm becoming overweight *and* I will eat pretzels instead of potato chips."

From Stevie Ray, a teacher of improvisational theater, I learned the creative power of saying "yes, and" instead of "yes, but" when responding to a new idea. "Yes, and" gives positive chemistry to a creative drama or conversation, while "yes, but" gives an adverse chemistry that closes down creative drama or meaningful interaction. The way we use language can open up possibilities or shut them down in an instant. Often the difference lies in a single word.

Move from monologues to dialogue

Almost anyone raised on a farm knows that cattle *ruminate.* That is, they chew the cud, bringing up an undigested gulp of food over and over again until it's ready for final swallowing. For cattle, rumination is necessary for digestion.

Human beings ruminate also, but we do it with our thoughts. This habit usually leads to mental indigestion. Cognitive psychologists use the word *rumination* when referring to someone who repeatedly says or thinks the same negative things. Maybe you know people who spend a lot of time alone nursing grudges, plotting revenge for imagined wrongs, or mentally replaying painful scenes from the past. Rumination of this type has some natural consequences, including bitterness, resentment, depression, and isolation.

Using the language of the theater, we can say that these people are stuck on a long interior monologue, one that adds up to miserable chemistry. They spend so much time talking to themselves that they rarely talk to others. The solution is to build more conversation into their roles, to write scripts that take them more outward than inward. Doing so allows the ruminators to stop chewing the

ACT NOW!

same old mental cud and make some real connections with other people.

The suggestions in this chapter are primarily about adding up-beat lines to your script. But at times we all must clear the chaff from our scripts—those unnecessary, unhealthy, pessimistic lines and thoughts.

When it comes to promoting health, it's important to reduce the cholesterol that clogs our arteries *and* to clear out the beliefs that clog our thinking. This means letting go of the ruminating negative thoughts and judgments about ourselves and others. Instead re-right the script, thinking "WE"-llcoming thoughts about others and pos"I"tive thoughts about yourself.

Choose thoughts and actions that will script you for an endorphin-raising upbeat role. Rehearse the modified script until it becomes a habit—until it becomes first nature—and you will have produced a chemistry that will enhance health and happiness.

"Shed the burden of judgment—you will feel much lighter," writes Deepak Chopra, author of *Ageless Mind, Timeless Body.* "Cleaning up the environment and getting rid of the toxic dumps and wastes that contaminate our earth, its rivers, and its oceans is worthwhile, but even more important is flushing out the toxic ideas that contaminate the human mind."

SCENE SEVEN

....

PRODUCE

A producer is someone who brings together all the human and financial elements needed for a performance. Producers ask these questions:

- Who will make up the *cast* for this play?

- Are we adequately *capitalized*—that is, do we have enough money to fund this production?

- Are we doing enough to direct and *cultivate* our actors' talents?

These are questions for all of us. In this chapter I offer answers to each one, along with some related suggestions.

Cast

Producers may spend months casting a performance. They know how crucial it is to choose a group of actors who operate as a harmonious ensemble on stage. After all, the feeling chemistry that a play generates in an audience will depend on how the cast interacts. Like actors on stage, we often match the thoughts, actions, and feeling chemistry of those with whom we associate.

ACT NOW!

Think for a moment about the people who share your stage at home, in the community, at school, or at work. Are you surrounding yourself with a positive, happy, healthy cast—people who listen well, carefully and caringly observe what you do, and support you as you act in line with your objectives? If not, think again about how you're producing your personal performance.

I suggest that you pick your cast with health and enjoyment in mind. Look for people who will help you generate the chemistry of an "on" performance. Sometimes this means avoiding negative, depressed people—those who drain you of physical and mental energy.

This is not always easy. "How can I pick and choose my cast members?" people ask me. "There are some real 'down' people who share my stage, and they happen to be members of my family or people I work with every day. I can't just get rid of them."

That's right. Few of us can "fire" our family members or put friends on probation. Even so, we can add more "sparklers" to our cast and focus our time and energy on these people. For every "downer" in your cast, see if you can "hire" some exciting new friends or contacts.

Another common question is, "What can I do about my husband who is always grumpy, always glum, always unhappy? How do I get him to change?" This reminds me of the woman who was asked, "Do you wake up grumpy in the morning?" "No," she replied, "I let him sleep." My approach is to downplay changing him. Instead, change yourself. Rewrite your own script to include some new lines and actions. Change what you say and do in response to your husband's grumpiness and unhappiness.

Where to start? Begin by setting an example. Model the kind of behavior you want him to adopt. Act up a little. Smile more. Laugh more. These simple behaviors are highly contagious and liable to lead to a "happy-demic." Also connect with new people. Talk about new ideas. Master the computer and teach him how to network with on-line techies. Bring some fresh influences into your relationship. Why wait for him to change when you can change your own script right now?

Marriage counselors often advise couples to act *as if* they're in love, knowing that the chemistry of romance can be rekindled in this way. This play may not seem real at first, but those who stay with the act often rewrite their relationship script. (For more ideas along these lines, I recommend the books *1001 Ways to Be Romantic* and *Romance 101: Lessons in Love* by Gregory Godek.)

In short, act as a catalyst who inspires a new chemistry for your relationship. You may have to pretend at first, and that's fine. The lines and actions you now find awkward and unfamiliar can become a habit with time and repetition. Just think of yourself as rehearsing a new part, one that will also call forth the finest performance from your fellow players. Skilled leaders in business, education, and government do this all the time.

Capitalize

In addition to casting, producers handle money matters. If you want happy actors, then you need to meet the payroll and pay the rent for the hall. If your production is undercapitalized, you can end up with empty seats in the theater and a short run for your play.

Likewise, when it comes to promoting health and happiness, I urge my audiences to learn about handling money wisely. I'm intrigued by the many connections between health and wealth. Both depend on how you spend your time and energy. The dividends you reap in both areas depend on conservation and stewardship of your

....

resources and building a reserve cushion of wealth, health, and happiness to fall back on.

Trainers in business and industry grab on to the wealth-health connection more readily than people in health education. If you attend enough seminars on how to be a better salesperson or a better manager, you'll eventually hear about exercise, diet, and stress management.

Business trainers know that financial and career success calls for managing your health resources. All of us need mental, emotional, and physical fuel to perform our parts at work with flair. I am pleased to note that master motivators such as Tony Robbins and Zig Ziglar agree on this point: Taking care of your mental and physical health sets the stage for greater wealth.

George Valliant, a Harvard psychologist, studied the health-wealth connection over a period of decades. In the process, he added another variable to the equation—humor. Using standard personality measures (such as the Myers-Briggs Inventory and Minnesota Multiphasic Personality Inventory), Valliant assigned a value to his subjects' *HQ*. Yes, that's *HQ*, not *IQ*.

While *IQ* stands for intelligence quotient, *HQ* refers to *humor quotient*. Valliant's high-HQ subjects were Harvard students with a "high serum fun level." These were the people other students loved to be around, the people most likely to get invitations for lunch, study groups, and parties.

Valliant followed these subjects for over three decades. He found that the high-HQ students enjoyed greater health and higher lifetime earnings compared to their lower-HQ classmates. Valliant concluded that higher-HQ subjects were more likely to be hired and promoted. What's more, people with high HQ ratings during college tended to maintain a high HQ throughout their careers.

....

Most of the lower-HQ students retained their HQ levels also, with corresponding results in health and wealth. Fortunately, some of the low-HQ students developed techniques to change their humor chemistry and approach the health and wealth level of their high-HQ classmates.

It's comforting to know that a few of the low HQers were able to re-right their script—to turn it around and get into a new act. They produce a chemistry that eventually enabled them, too, to appreciate the physiological applause of wealth, health, and happiness.

Smile your way to success

Smiling is one of the easiest ways to get into the act of success. I like to quote a study done for a restaurant chain that sent its food servers to "smile school"—customer service training. During this training, food servers learned how to be overly nice to their customers. They were openly encouraged to wear a syrupy grin and be overly solicitous of clients. In short, they were told to put on a friendly act.

A survey of customers who later encountered these employees revealed some fascinating results. These customers did not resent the employees' attitudes or actions. In fact, many of them appreciated the overly nice approach of the food servers. And that appreciation led to financial generosity. Customers rewarded the servers who'd been to smile school with a 27 percent increase in tips.

The more I think about this study, the less I find these results surprising. Most of us like to do business with people who are smilers. We describe them as friendly, outgoing, warm, and gregarious. We gravitate to these endorphin raisers in stores, offices, and schools. These are the employees who know how to generate a personal chemistry that we enjoy.

If the health and wealth connection is hard for you to buy, then consider another idea: Poor finances can create the chemistry of poor health. While working in orthopedic medicine and seeing people with back pain, I learned that many of my patients were going through some kind of financial crisis. These crises triggered fear, anger, and other emotions that threw certain muscles of their lower backs into gridlock.

I've seen a surprisingly large number of patients in chronic pain who have experienced fear and anger related to serious financial difficulties. Many of these people were deeply in debt and some were fending off creditors like wolves from the door. Few of these patients took the time to adequately chart their financial future or set aside money for emergency expenses. They simply failed to capitalize. Eventually they felt the painful chemistry of a disappointing financial "curtain call." And they had no "material" to put on an encore. The hurting of their finances manifested in the aches and pains of the body.

Your prescription for financial security

There is no sure-fire formula for capitalizing, but I'll give you five suggestions for taking immediate hold of your financial future—10 words total. These suggestions don't take up much space on this page, yet they capture the basics of sound money management:

- Spend less.

- Earn more.

- Save more.

- Invest wisely.

- Don't gamble.

That's it. If you can put these five ideas into practice, you'll go a long way toward capitalizing in grand style. Succeeding at financial management doesn't take genius. It takes only a modicum of discipline and the ability to add and subtract.

Start with spending less. My suggested treatment for the the many bodily pains that stem from financial illness is not more doctoring and medication but financial counseling. I recommend that patients with money pains lower their spending. My goal for them is to free up 5 to 10 percent of their income for saving, investing, and reducing debts. In high school and college this message should be part of health class, right up there with sex education.

For many this is a hard pill to swallow. Yet the arithmetic is inescapable: If your outgo exceeds your income, then your upkeep will be your downfall! Too many people with chronic pain have a habit of spending 105, 110, or 120 percent or more of their income. They have no savings—no cushion for a soft landing after sudden, unforeseen expenses. In effect they deposit their fears and anger in a bank of tight muscles, and the dividend is paid out in aches and pains.

Take a larger view of wealth

I do not want to leave you with the impression that health requires a large bank account. Wealth has a tangible element—the amount of money you have. Yet the intangibles—satisfaction with your work, an enduring sense of purpose, stable relationships—are just as important. Many of us know people with minimal monetary means who feel rich. And we know moneyed people who feel and are poor. Those who are inwardly rich use available props to set their stage and enjoy their present setting. At the same time, they consistently work toward improving their role for tomorrow's performance.

I associate the word *wealth* with many riches that can't be count-ed—a wealth of pleasant emotion, a wealth of friends, and a healthy surge of the chemicals that boost our immune system. Anyone who believes in what you're doing and offers emotional or spiritual support is helping you capitalize.

Cultivate

At some point, each of us sits in the director's chair. We supervise others. We raise children. We play leadership roles in our commu-nity. These are just a few examples of the directing that takes place on the various stages of daily life.

Knowing this, you can consciously take on the director's role when the time comes and perform the part with grace and skill. Cultivating the talents of others through coaching and teaching is a powerful way to connect with people.

In medical school I learned strategies for enforcing "patient com-pliance." I heard about ways to shame, cajole, or threaten patients into following my prescriptions and instructions. As a young doc-tor in practice, however, I found this approach frustrating, and its record of success bears out my early impressions.

Today I'd rather talk about scripting our patients or helping them accept direction. I'd rather see myself as a coach, a director, or even a prompter than as a policeman. I want to cast people as the star of their own production and myself as part of their supporting cast.

Much of our job as directors (parents, friends, or teachers) is not to teach techniques but to convey attitudes. Today we grandparents are less likely to teach kids how to fish than to teach the value of fishing by demonstrating a feeling of pleasure. This represents a big change for people of my generation. As I was growing up, a grandfather would teach me how to milk a cow, build a birdhouse, and do some basic carpentry. In those days, older people were wiser because they passed on specific skills to members of the younger generation.

I know my grandchildren will teach *me* about computers, cars, and digital stereo equipment. They will be more current with the skills required to run our advanced technology. That leaves me to teach the timeless skills of temperament and attitude. These are the skills of finding pleasure in work and family life, the skills of connecting with and contributing to other people, the skills of laughing and lingering in the sun and acting lazy when the time comes. These are the skills of inspiring the chemistry of love, hope, and happiness—the joy of just doing and being.

Of course, I could also teach my grandchildren how to complain, how to see themselves as victims of circumstance, or how to mistrust others and maintain that the world is going to hell in a handbasket. What determines the lessons I pass on is the example I set. Children learn from us during every second they spend in our company. We teach the skills of temperament in a simple yet profound way—by demonstrating those skills in thought, word, and action. Directing others, then, starts with directing yourself.

There also comes a time for us to accept direction from the outside. Our directors in life are many—parents, friends, family members, physicians, teachers, coaches, mentors, and sponsors. Being open to their direction means listening with full attention, accepting criticism, approaching new ideas with an open mind, and changing our behavior. We need to be open to seeing ourselves as others see us.

Too much of our time as listeners is spent on searching for what's wrong with other people's ideas. We listen for the 10 percent or the 5 percent or the 1 percent of the message that we disagree with. We spend too little time accentuating and building on our areas of agreement. Instead, we could listen with several questions in mind: What's right about this idea? What is potentially useful about this viewpoint? How about giving this suggestion a try and seeing if it makes a difference?

The notion of accepting direction offers us a way to talk common sense about spirituality. Spirituality is a rich word with many dimensions of meaning. Among other things, spirituality means discovering our true nature, connecting with a caring community of people, and finding a purpose in life that goes beyond short-term concerns.

In addition, I see spirituality as *accepting ultimate direction.* You can give any name you want to the source of that direction—God, higher power, greater intelligence, intuition, inner guide, or many others. The name we use is less important than our willingness to accept direction from a source of wisdom that goes beyond our everyday mind. This is a prime source of the chemistry of health and happiness.

I often tell audiences—particularly religious groups—that humans have been created with the God-given chemistry of health and happiness. These chemicals are raised by many healthy pleasures, one of which is the rapture felt during religious experiences such as meditation and prayer. The chemicals that move us emotionally during these religious experiences are probably related to the endorphins. Remember that endorphins are the inner uppers the chemicals that get us high on life.

As a sophomore at Carleton College I considered entering the ministry until I read a line from Karl Marx that changed my mind. Marx wrote that "Religion is the opiate of the people." That quote bothered me a great deal then, leading to several nights of fitful sleep and then a decision to follow another vocational path.

But today, as my medical colleagues unravel the mysteries of psychoneuroimmunology, I realize that indeed the chemistry of good health and the chemistry of religion can converge.

Perhaps Marx was prophetic in a way he never imagined. Perhaps there is a divinely inspired, health-promoting chemistry that is enhanced by being spiritually directed.

Church leaders preach how those who are born again change their chemistry. They develop a healthy script and act. And health statistics show that those who follow a spiritual script (no matter what the religion) enjoy the wealth of personal satisfaction and increased longevity. I still recall the words of my grandma: "Dale, if you're going to be a good Christian, you better start acting like a good Christian!" Taking her statement a step further, we could say "If you're going to be good at anything, you better start acting the part!"

Give, receive, and expect pleasure

If I could pass on any one piece of wisdom to my cast members, it would be this: Pleasure is good. I do not mean the shallow, one-shot pleasures, like getting drunk or gorging on food. Instead I refer to the deep-seated and enduring pleasures: life-long friendships, caring for others, creative work, art, and music. Great producers and directors love to give pleasure. They also expect pleasure. Simply by virtue of showing up for the performance, they feel they have a right to enjoy the play.

This is one of the most profound lessons we can teach our children and grandchildren: It is OK to enjoy ourselves and others. It is OK to please ourselves and to please others. I want my children and

ACT NOW!

grandchildren to receive and give healthy pleasures, even if it's just in small doses—a smile, greeting card, flower, sincere compliment, or loving touch.

We can teach our children how to exercise, eat wisely, and make choices that promote a lifetime of health. Yet it's just as important to teach them to regularly smile, laugh, and shamelessly raise their endorphin levels in a myriad of other ways. Healthy pleasures are our birthright. Let us pass them on to our descendants. Our "understudies" will mimic our words and deeds, so let's give them a script for happiness and health.

Children learn attitudes and beliefs the same way they learn a language—by imitation. It has been said that,

> *No written word or mortal plea*
> *Can teach young hearts what they should be;*
> *Nor all the books upon the shelves,*
> *But what the teachers are themselves.*

Children absorb not only the spoken word, but the attitudes and feeling chemistries produced in their families.

I invite you to fill your life with healthy pleasures. By doing so you will help to change the feeling chemistries generated in our society, and the rest of us will benefit from your good work.

I implore parents and grandparents to teach optimism by being optimistic. Let us teach our children and our grandchildren that they are born into an endorphin-raising culture where smiling is the most frequent form of communication. Let us teach these things by example—even if we have to fake it at first! Let us teach our children that the language of fun and laughter is fluently spoken in our homes—and that it's good to laugh just for the health of it.

SCENE EIGHT
....

MOVE

"Movements disclose a person's interests, tastes, habits, moods," notes Sonia Moore in her book *The Stanislavski System: The Professional Training of an Actor.* "The complex of human psychological life is expressed through a simple physical action."

Those two sentences sum up volumes about Stanislavski's Method. Over and over again, Stanislavski pointed to the importance of movement in revealing an actor's feelings. A simple glance, a raised eyebrow, the hint of a smile—even these small, subtle movements can give clues to an ocean of feeling that lies beneath the actor's surface appearance.

Movement changes chemistry

Each of us has a complicated "vocabulary" of gestures associated with key emotions—gestures of anger, of love, of sadness, of joy, and more. It is the actor's job to learn this vocabulary. On stage, Stanislavski said, actors become children. That is, they learn to move, gesture, and speak all over again. Under the glare of stage lights and the gaze of an audience, they find that even the simplest

• •

actions can become forced and strained. Actors can become so self-conscious that they forget how to walk, sit, breathe, or stand. The solution is learning to move all over again in harmony with the characters they are to create.

Stanislavski said that acting is like traveling. On stage every actor embarks on a journey toward the character's super-objective. That journey consists of a trail of actions played out in scene after scene. Movement, noted Stanislavski, builds a "track" that takes characters from their present state to their ultimate goal. It is every actor's job to trace that trail of actions in fine detail.

The more recent literature on body language confirms this idea. "Our first impressions of others are almost always formed within the first two to four minutes of meeting them," writes David Lewis, a consultant who coaches people on using effective body language. "During this time we are concentrating less on what is being said and more on the other person's facial expressions, gazes, gestures, posture, stance, and proximity." Actors who study the Method create their characters by attending to these kinds of details.

According to John Grinder and Richard Bandler, the founders of neurolinguistic programming, even the smallest movement of our eyes is a window to our inner world. People who learn best through charts, diagrams, and other visuals often move their eyes upward, especially when trying to visually reconstruct a memory. In contrast, people with an auditory learning style often move their eyes to the side (toward their ears) when processing new information. And kinesthetic learners—those who acquire new skills by taking action—usually cast their eyes downward (toward the torso) while learning.

According to drama coach Max Dixon, right-handed dramatists who are trying to memorize or recall their lines move their eyes upward and to the right. When envisioning a role, they look upward

• •

and to the left. When attempting to hear the scene, they gaze to the side, and when rekindling the emotional chemistry of a part their eyes move downward and to the left.

In summary, all body movement reveals thought and feeling. At the same time, movement can change the way we think and feel because it changes our biochemistry. Feelings and chemistry are one and the same.

Recently I came across an exciting new word that points to this idea—*cyberphysiology*. *Cyber* comes from a word that means "to steer" and refers to movement, while *physiology* connotes chemistry. Cyberphysiology, then, is "movement chemistry," or the study of how deliberate movement affects mind-body chemistry.

Cyberphysiology and other alternative healthcare approaches are being explored by the Archaeus Project, a mind-body think tank spearheaded by Earl Bakken, founder and retired CEO of Medtronic, Inc. Bakken has been a guiding light to the health care industry. He helped lead medicine into the modern high-tech era, and now he and the Archaeus project are reaching out to help healthcare regain and understand the benefits of high touch.

At the heart of cyberphysiology is a simple suggestion: If you want to change the way you feel, then change the way you move—the way you steer your actions.

Condition yourself through conducting

Stanislavski constantly reminded his students that mental and physical conditioning are essential for a great performance. The tools of the actor's trade are the human body and mind. Honing

those tools called concentration, observation, muscular strength, and physical endurance are the starting points for any "on" performance.

The actor's instrument is the human body. Just as musicians work to keep their instruments in working order, we can hone our physical and mental health so that our bodies stay in shape for a lifetime of performances.

Conditioning brings us to the subject of exercise. Volumes have been written and spoken on this subject, and my purpose is not to summarize that literature here. However, I will recommend a simple, effective form of exercise that's a little different than most. I call it *J'ARMing*, which is short for "jogging with the arms." J'ARMing is an exercise that will help us get in tune with the rhythms of life.

It was George, a delightful retired line worker who said to me when he was 67 years old, "I know I need more exercise. But with my bad hips, it's painful to jog. I don't like swimming, and I feel self-conscious at the health clubs with all those trim, beautiful, perspiring young women putting the rush on me." (George had a vivid imagination.) He also spoke of the three M's that made him shy away from health clubs: machines, mirrors, and massive muscles.

George recalled as a young man in his 20s that he was "trim and fit as a fiddle." Back then, he and his wife did a lot of dancing, and he even worked for a few years as a band director and sang in a barbershop quartet. "Those were the active good old days, Doc. Never felt better. Music around me, music within me. Just the memory of those times strikes up the band in my mind."

Profound, I thought, as I listened to George. He brought to mind the words of Oliver Wendell Holmes: "Too many people die with their music in them."

"How did it feel to be a conductor?" I asked.

George thought for a moment. Then he told me how healthy and happy he felt when he was actively conducting. "You know, it was kind of like jogging—with the arms," he said. Ever since then, I've used the word *J'ARMing* to describe the exercise you get from imitating the movements of conductors.

George's comment was the seed for a harvest of health benefits for him, as it can be for you. Professional conductors know about the benefits of J'ARMing, even if they don't use the term. Great symphony orchestra conductors tend to live longer—an average of five years longer, in fact—than the general population. They also are said to be healthier in both mind and body than many others in their age group.

In 1980, the Metropolitan Life Insurance Company published the results of a study on the longevity of conductors. Researchers looked at the life spans of 437 active and former conductors of regional and community orchestras across America. The conclusion: Mortality among symphony conductors was 38 percent below their contemporaries in the general population.

For example, Toscanini died just two months and two days before his 90th birthday. Leopold Stokowski lived to be 95. Arthur Fiedler was 85, and Bruno Walter was 86. Even Leonard Bernstein, who died at the relatively young age of 72, beat the odds. "God knows, I should be dead by now," Bernstein remarked a couple of years before his death. "I smoke. I drink. I stay up all night. I'm overcommitted on all fronts. I was told that if I didn't stop smoking, I'd be dead at 35. Well, I beat the rap."

One of the things that helps these people beat the rap is the sheer fun of conducting—making those grand, sweeping motions of the arms surrounded by an ocean of musical sound. There's a large element of play in conducting. "You can't be serious 24 hours a day. You have to take half-an-hour or an hour a day to be childish," said pianist Vladimir Horowitz. "Conducting is a real sport," noted composer Aaron Copland. "You can never guarantee what the results are going to be, so there's always an element of chance. That keeps it exciting."

We can't say there is a direct cause-and-effect relationship between conducting movements and living into one's 80s or 90s. Other factors are probably at work—among them, commitment to a vocation, connection to other people, and a passion for music. Yet the correlation between conducting and health in these people is striking.

Many of us can fondly recall times when, as children, we captured something of the excitement these great musicians must feel. At those times, we directed music naturally. We threw our arms up in the air with childlike abandon and marched around, moving to the music. Some of us even pretended we were leading a large orchestra as we stood in front of a mirror. Many of us who see a conductor at work have to fight back the urge once again to become like a child and mimic those movements. We'd love to let go and allow our bodies to flow with the music.

J'ARMing gives you the excuse. The idea behind J'ARMing is to let yourself go, become childlike, regress a little bit, and at the same time regenerate both your mind and your body. You lift a baton and play the part of a conductor, band leader, or choir director. As you do this, you can recapture that childlike excitement, that feeling of being in control and of leaving stress and pain behind.

I encourage everyone to J'ARM. At the end of my speaking programs, I always include a short J'ARMing session. I pass out special J'ARM sticks (chopsticks, actually) and play upbeat, lively songs to which the audience and I J'ARM. Audiences always get their arms moving to the music. Soon they are laughing, marching, and conducting themselves in a healthy, carefree manner, enjoying themselves in a way that many haven't experienced in years. Many reportedly continue to carry on and "strike up the band" at home and work.

Basic J'ARMing

J'ARMing is a unique exercise. First off, there are many things you do *not* need to J'ARM. You need no fancy clothing, no expensive shoes, no elaborate equipment, no special building, gym, or exercise facility. You need not learn any special technique, because you develop your own unique style. You can J'ARM anywhere, with or without clothing. (Careful with the latter option!)

You can J'ARM at any time, no appointments necessary. Nor do you need special lighting. In fact, you can J'ARM in the dark. You do not need a score board. No grades are given. Bad weather need not keep you from J'ARMing. Dogs won't nip at your heels, cars won't honk at or splash on you, and no salesperson will call to sell you a membership. To paraphrase Dr. Seuss:

You can J'ARM in a park.

You can J'ARM in the dark.

You can J'ARM as a lark.

You can J'ARM in a chair.

You can J'ARM on the stair.

You can even J'ARM in the bare!

You can J'ARM here or there.

You can J'ARM anywhere!

In J'ARM 101 there are only two simple suggestions to follow. First, get your arms moving and don't worry about how you look. Sometimes beginning J'ARMers worry about looking silly. So look silly! What form of exercise doesn't look a little silly, anyway?

Second, choose some upbeat, invigorating music to go along with your arm movements. Music with uplifting lyrics is ideal, because the positive message helps raise those "inner uppers," the endorphins. This is all you need to get started.

Intermediate J'ARMing

After several sessions of basic J'ARMing, you may want to move on to the intermediate course. Now that you have mastered the basics, you can begin to exaggerate your arm and body movements—provided it's not painful to do so. Move your arms more vigorously, lift them higher, and widen the arc of your movements. If you feel inclined, and if you've checked with your physician about doing so, you may want to add weights to your arms. Runners often use such weights, and you can generally find them in sports supply stores.

Next, devote some more attention to the music you're using. Again, each J'ARMer will have her own favorite type of music. It may be classical, pop, jazz, country western, religious, golden oldies, or Gregorian chants. Choose what feels right, whatever gives *you* an inner feeling of harmony. My only recommendation is that you J'ARM to a variety of music. That keeps the program fresh, as well as educational. (For more ideas, see my suggestions for music" on page 172.)

I'd also like you to experiment with singing as you J'ARM. Those who sing seem to experience some special good vibrations. Vibrations of the voice may have special healing properties. Songs and chants are an important part of the ceremonies in almost all religions, and they're widely used to calm the body and center the mind. It's possible that the body "reads" these vibrations on a deep, chemical level. In some sacred traditions, singing is used to connect people with their natural surroundings, their fellow human beings, and their creator.

At the every least, singing increases the aerobic effect of J'ARMing. When you sing, you get more aerobic exercise, and you just might have more fun. Incidentally, don't worry if you're J'ARMing to orchestral or other instrumental music without words. Just sing along with the melody using simple syllables such as "la," or "da," or make up your own lyrics. And if you don't feel like singing, whistle! Whatever you do, make noise. Be loud. Live it up!

Advanced J'ARMing

Unlike the conductors you see in concert halls or on television, you will not be confined to a small riser or platform when you conduct. Don't you feel sorry for conductors when the music almost shouts "move!" and they have to control themselves to maintain an artistic composure? Imagine how the audience might react if a conductor would suddenly leap off the podium and dance or march across the stage!

Aren't you lucky that you have no such worries to contend with? And isn't it comforting to realize you don't have any talented artistic image to uphold? For me, having little or no talent can be a decided advantage. What I lack in musical talent I can make up for in spirited movement.

So if you can, move across the room when you J'ARM. You don't have to stay in a confined space. One of my fantasies is to J'ARM in a large dance hall or auditorium, with music from the sound system filling the whole place. As I J'ARM, I stroll, walk, dance, march, leap, jog, or even run from one end of the place to another. And there's nobody there to stop me or even notice what I'm doing.

You can do something like this at home. Feel free to move anywhere in your home, as long as you can still hear the music. J'ARM while moving from room to room or floor to floor. You'll just burn more calories as you do so.

Another simple but effective variation is to step up and step down on a step while J'ARMing. Or walk up and down stairs as you J'ARM. Both methods increase the aerobic benefit and develop the upper leg and hip muscles.

Another variation is to J'ARM using a chair. Sit down in the chair, and then rise from the seated position. Sit again. Then rise again. Keep repeating these movements, and keep your arms moving to the music the whole time. This is one exercise that helps keep VP's (vintage people) living independently. It builds muscles in the upper leg and groin area—the muscles we use to sit down, stand up, and walk. Such up-down, up-down exercise keeps the "get up and go" muscles strong.

If you're feeling really adventuresome, experiment with J'ARMing while sitting in a rocking chair. A few well balanced J'ARMers have conducted on a rocker board they purchased in a sporting goods or physical therapy store.

But rocker boards are out of the question for most of us, so just standing on one leg can help develop and maintain the sense of balance. This exercise makes use of your proprioceptors—the nerve endings that determine your orientation in space. Persons with good proprioceptors are usually better coordinated and less likely to fall. If they do fall, they are better able to steer their fall and experience a soft landing. Proprioception diminishes with time unless these nerves are maintained with use.

All these are just optional suggestions. If you do add such movements to your J'ARMing program, start slowly and allow time for a warm-up at the beginning of each J'ARMing session. Above all, remember that the point of J'ARMing is to "conduct yourself well" while having more fun than you can "shake a stick at."

Face the music

Listening to music offers a potent way to alter our moods and spark the healing chemistry of good feeling. One of the enduring pleasures of life is discovering a piece of music that strikes a personal chord, lifts your spirits, raises you up, and improves your chemistry.

To increase your chances of experiencing that pleasure over and over again, stay open to all kinds of music. If you're a die-hard classical fan, sample some Duke Ellington. If you swear by polkas, go out on a limb and try some Vivaldi. And even if you swoon at the voice of Pavorotti, be willing to put some early Beatles recordings in your music player.

Forget the labels—jazz, classical, rock, country-western, and all the rest. Musicians today, especially pop artists, borrow from many styles as they create. The labels we grew up with may no longer yield an accurate map of the musical territory. A variety of music can keep your J'ARM program interesting.

Keep in mind, too, that music associated with certain occasions or times of the year can be suitable for listening year-round. You can enjoy holiday music anytime, as well as the music played during the central events in your life—weddings, bar mitzvahs, birthdays, and other celebrations.

When you ask people to recommend music that calms and uplifts the spirit, some of them may mention so-called "new age" recordings. Some people I know react negatively to that term, as I did at first. Don't let the term scare you away. New age is a broad term that now encompasses something for just about everyone—everything from Bach to light jazz.

If you poke around the new age bins in music stores, you may well find something you like. One advantage of doing so is that many of the people interested in creating, recording, and distributing this music are especially interested in the effects of music on the human psyche and body. Their work therefore meshes with the ideas in this book.

I recommend that you adopt a daily diet of uplifting music. This regimen is calorie-free. Paired with J'ARMing, the health benefits it yields can last a lifetime. One place to start is with *any* recordings of simple, upbeat popular tunes such as these:

"Smile"

"Put on a Happy Face"

"This Land Is Your Land"

"The Happy Wanderer"

"Hail, Hail the Gang's All Here"

"Happiness Is"

"Oh, What a Beautiful Morning"

"On the Sunny Side of The Street"

"Happy Days Are Here Again"

"If I Had a Hammer"

"Smiles"

"Keep Young at Heart"

"Mickey Mouse March"

"The More We Get Together"

"Oh When the Saints Go Marching In"

Also J'ARM to music from your favorite cartoons, television shows, and film soundtracks. This could range from "The Sound of Music" or "The Music Man" to the themes from "I Love Lucy" or "The Dick Van Dyke Show." If your high school days were filled with fond memories, you may find the music from that decade particularly satisfying. Listen to a collection of favorites from your adolescent decade to recall some of your youthful chemistry of that period. For more recommended music, see the Discography on page 221.

Move your mind

By learning how to J'ARM, you explore physical conditioning. Another kind of exercise is equally important: mental conditioning.

Mental conditioning becomes especially important as people grow older. To understand why, remember that we really have three distinct ages: a chronological age, a physiological age, and a mental age. Anyone who still has a birth certificate can verify his or her chronological age—the number of years and days that person has lived. That's fairly straightforward.

Physiological age is a more subtle concept, however. This age has a lot to do with one's state of health. During the first months of his presidency, George Bush underwent a physical examination. He was 65 at the time, but his physician said that he had the physical condition of a man of 55. This fact is not surprising, since we know that Bush worked out to maintain a slim-fit physique and had a regular exercise regimen. Former President Bush gives us an example of how physiological age can prevail over chronological age, the inexorable march of passing years.

ACT NOW!

That brings us to the third concept, mental age. Here we could profit from studying the lives of the great comedians—not those who burned out or died young because of destructive lifestyle choices, but those who used humor to keep themselves perennially young at heart.

One of my favorite examples is George Burns. Once someone asked him if he had a happy childhood. "So far," was his reply. At Burns' 85th birthday party, another person asked him how it felt to be 85. "When I feel 85," he said, "I'll let you know." Soon, on his 100th birthday, Burns is scheduled to play the Palladium Theater in London. What a fantastic role model he is for all VP's (Vintage People)!

Another person who comes to mind is Satchel Paige, the great baseball player and legendary pitcher. Paige was black, and racial discrimination barred him from the major leagues until relatively late in his career. By the time he joined the Cleveland Indians in 1948, Paige was already older than most of the other players. Add to this the fact that Paige really didn't know his chronological age. No one could remember his exact birth date, and he didn't have a birth certificate. According to some reports, not even Paige's mother could remember exactly when he was born.

There grew a kind of mystique about this whole matter. Reporters, awed at Paige's prowess on the baseball field, kept asking him how old he was. Once Paige lost his patience and turned the tables on an inquiring reporter by firing back a single question: "Young man," he asked, "how old would you be if you didn't know how old you *was*?"

That question is relevant to all of us. It reminds us that we don't have to act according to anyone's preconceived notions about what people are supposed to act like at age 60, 70, or 80. Throw away the stereotypes about aging, and discourage the jokes about age that dwell on loss of various mental and bodily functions.

Move

Pretend for a moment that your birth certificate has been lost forever and no one has a clue to the day and year you entered the world. How old do you feel or *want* to feel right now? How much energy do you have or *want* to have to accomplish the things that matter? What projects and goals are you actively pursuing? What activities imbue your life with a sense of passion and purpose? Would knowing your chronological age make any difference in all this?

Please consider putting on the mental costume of a younger age. Set your stage, costume, and script for an age that you can make real. Then, and only then, act your age.

Breathe!

Any effective form of physical conditioning works with the basic motion that sustains human life—the movement of air in and out of our lungs. In addition, breathing may offer the most direct way to alter your emotional state.

During my stint as an emergency room physician, I sometimes saw people in a state of near panic—agitated, deeply upset, even afraid they were going to die. At the same time, they were usually hyperventilating (taking rapid, shallow breaths). This significantly altered the oxygen-carbon dioxide balance of their lung gases; they had too much oxygen and too little carbon dioxide. Often my first instruction to these patients was to slow down their breathing or to breathe into a paper bag. Immediately this simple act helped to restore their presence of mind and calm their runaway emotions.

I probably first learned about the power of slowing the breath when, as a child, I was instructed to count sheep to help me fall asleep. Of course, teachings about the power of breathing predate me by thousands of years. The ancient discipline of yoga includes a

ACT NOW!

series of breathing exercises known as *pranayama*. Similar practices exist in other ancient religions and healing arts.

Breathing may be as significant to health as diet or exercise. As Andrew Weil notes in *Natural Health, Natural Medicine*, "You cannot be upset if your breathing is slow, deep, quiet, and regular. You cannot always center yourself emotionally by an act of will, but you can use your voluntary nerves to make your breathing, slow, deep, quiet, and regular, and the rest will follow."

Experience this for yourself with a simple breathing exercise that Weil recommends:

1. Place the tip of your tongue behind your upper front teeth and keep it there for the rest of the exercise.

2. Exhale completely through your mouth, making a *woosh* sound.

3. Close your mouth and inhale quietly to a mental count of four.

4. Hold your breath while counting to seven.

5. Exhale completely through your mouth again, making a *woosh* sound as you count to eight.

This completes one cycle of the exercise. Doing just two or three cycles will help you relax even when you feel most stressed.

Now matter how they're presented, most meditation methods depend on the slowing of the breath, often with a formula which involves inhaling for a certain count, holding for a longer count, and then exhaling for an even longer count. Whatever the formula, the common denominator is a change in respiratory physiological chemistry.

Meditate!

As I learn about the mind-body connection, I realize how important it is for us to investigate the various schools of meditation. And I include meditation here in the Move Scene because I feel that the most important element of meditation is the act of breathing. Breath control seems to be the ticket to the chemistry of successful meditation. While thought, centering, and scripting are obviously involved, it's the breathing that changes the chemistry.

The meditation literature offers a rich theory and practice related to mind-body connection, one that goes back several thousand years. Today, under the guidance of the Stanislavski Method, actors also learn to focus and manage their attention, just as skilled meditators do.

My experiences with meditation have been varied. While meditating, I've learned to relax by painting a number of pleasant scenes in my mind. I've strolled down garden paths and walked by babbling brooks; I've glided up and down in mental elevators and climbed up and down stairs; I've inhaled through my fingers and exhaled through my toes. These are just a few examples. Many people find this kind of mental imagery helpful, and I recommend that you learn more about it. Just go to a library or bookstore and browse through the books on visualization. (In particular, look for the classic *Creative Visualization* by Shakti Gawain.)

There are many ways to activate healing chemistry through meditation and visualization. Choose the ones that work best for you.

When investigating subjects such as meditation, I find that it helps me to "hook" new information on to something I already know. For me, one of those mental hooks is chemistry. When you get right down to it, every style of meditation is a set of instructions for changing your mind-body chemistry. Now, the people who teach you meditation may not see it that way. They're more apt to talk about this powerful practice in more "highfalutin" terms, such as "getting in touch with your spirit" or opening up "channels in your body that let your energy flow freely."

I won't comment on those ideas here, but I will alert you to one claim that is a little fuzzy. Some meditators tout the virtues of meditation by saying that it moves more oxygen through your mind-body, just like aerobic exercise. In reality, most meditation practices do just the opposite; they *slow* your breathing. When this happens, you actually absorb less oxygen—not more—and you retain carbon dioxide.

The result is a new chemistry—specifically, a change in the acid–base (pH) balance of your mind-body. When you breathe more slowly, you retain more carbon dioxide. In turn, the increased carbon dioxide raises your levels of carbolic acid. You literally become more acidic. (If you've studied respiratory physiology, you may have heard about the Henderson–Hasselbalch equation, which describes this phenomenon.)

This change in chemistry will undoubtedly lead to a change in your feelings as well. As your chemistry becomes more "respiratory acidotic" every cell in the body is affected. Your muscles relax. You might even feel like going to sleep. At the same time, you may feel more attentive, more aware of your inner feelings, more "in tune" with yourself.

Meditation can be an effective method for reducing stress and gaining personal insight. If you're uncomfortable with the idea of a formal meditation practice, then just think in terms of slowing the breathing and of *mindfulness,* the essences of meditation.

Lately a whole crop of literature has sprung up around the power of mindfulness. (A wonderful book on the subject is *Full Catastrophe*

Living: Using the Wisdom of Your Body and Mind to Face Stress, Pain and Illness by Jon Kabat-Zinn.) By mindfulness I mean a deliberate, detailed, and nonjudgmental attention to whatever you are thinking, feeling, or doing in the present moment. This habit, when practiced regularly, has an uncanny power to relieve many symptoms of stress and restore mental perspective.

Thich Nhat Hanh, a Buddhist monk from Vietnam who was nominated by Martin Luther King for a Nobel Peace Prize, is also known for his simple, eloquent teachings on mindfulness.

In *The Miracle of Mindfulness: A Manual on Meditation,* Hanh offers many exercises as an aid to practicing mindfulness in daily life. Several of them use techniques that bring Stanislavski's ideas to mind. I recommend the following exercises of Thich Nhat Hanh for starters because they include one of my favorite practices—smiling:

• Take three slow, deep breaths the first thing upon waking in the morning. As you breathe in this way, smile a half-smile. Notice what happens to your emotional state as you do.

• Look at something beautiful, such as a child, painting, or flower. As you do, breathe slowly three times and half-smile. Consider the object of your attention as an aspect of yourself.

• Any time you feel angry or irritated, notice this feeling without judging it. Then half-smile immediately and breathe slowly three times.

Tai Chi, yoga, and related exercises also embrace mindfulness practice. In addition, they get you moving and can provide benefits similar to aerobic exercise.

ACT NOW!

Relax!

Stanislavski devoted a great deal of attention to relaxation. He noted that the mere act of walking on stage and performing in front of an audience promotes tension, stage fright, and even anxiety. As a result, actors must constantly search out points of muscular tension and consciously relax them, doing this so often that it becomes a habit.

Physical relaxation is essential for all of us as we play our parts in life. A person who's tense and anxious finds it difficult to perform well on any "stage." I'd guess that about 25 percent of the literature on wellness is about this single topic—how to relax.

Tension leads to forced and unnatural movement. Stanislavski had a colorful way of demonstrating this. He'd ask a group of his students to gather around a piano and then try to lift it while reciting their lines at the same time. Most found that the resulting physical and mental tension made it impossible to act.

Unfortunately, many of us hold unnecessary tension without realizing it. In turn, this leads to muscular aches that curtail the movements we need to perform well. Evidence of these aches comes in the form of tender knots of pain that tell us what we cannot do without pain. Mother Nature, however, has a system for scripting and costuming the body that will often rid it of these limitations. This is the subject of my book *Muscle Pain Relief in 90 Seconds: The Fold and Hold Method*, which details how aches can go away overnight when we learn to follow the intuitive prompting of our body-mind.

Students of the Method learn detailed techniques for relaxing. For example, Stanislavski often asked his students to assume a variety of poses and then describe, muscle by muscle, where they felt points of tension.

Move

I have used a similar approach to show how different unpleasant emotional chemistry can cause body aches and pains. For instance a "cartoon caricature" pose of fear or anger will quickly elicit pain in the lower back. And in a matter of seconds, the pose of being "time pressured," being "dumped on," or carrying the "weight of the world on the shoulders" will recreate or make worse upper back and neck pains.

This simple office demonstration helps patients understand that their emotional chemistry is the cause of or significantly contributes to their physical discomfort. And this chemistry is the result of how they have costumed, scripted, staged, and acted their life.

Many people in pain need to learn how to act more relaxed.

There are many simple ways to achieve states of profound relaxation. The following instructions are for an exercise from the yoga literature—the *savasana* pose. When done properly, this exercise can be as restorative as a nap:

1. Lie on your back with your arms at your sides. Adjust your body as needed to find the most comfortable position.

2. Notice your breathing. Don't try to change your rate of breathing. Instead, just become aware of your respiration and let your breathing assume its own pace. It will slow down naturally. Allow yourself to become very relaxed, even as you stay mentally alert.

3. Now become aware of each major part of your body to find out if it is truly relaxed. Begin with your feet. If you discover any tension in them, consciously relax them. Imagine that the tense muscles are melting like butter on a warm, sunny summer day.

4. Repeat step 3 as you progressively focus on other areas of your body: legs, abdomen, chest, fingers, forearms, upper arms, shoulders, and neck. Give special attention to the muscles of your face and forehead.

Repeat these four steps two or three times. If possible, devote a full half-hour to this exercise. Your mind-body will thank you every time!

In conclusion, Stanislavski might have said: "Actors will not give themselves up wholly to a role unless it carries them away. But if they become completely identified with the role they will be transformed. This capacity to transform oneself, body and soul, is the prime requirement for success *on* any stage, *in* any stage or *at* any stage in the "drama" of life. Act now!!"

SCENE NINE

....

REHEARSE

Our habits are everyday acts that to a large extent determine the chemistry of our health. Certain habits promote our well-being, while others undermine it.

Health hinges on habits

Most of this book is about making and breaking habits—opening new acts and closing old ones. We all have habits related to smiling, posture, breathing, relaxing, thinking, exercise, planning, and other topics.

All these habits have the potential to affect your thinking and your actions, thus triggering the healing chemistry spoken of in psychoneuroimmunology.

Oversimplifying things a bit, I say that healing is a matter of chemistry, and habits are chemistry. Behind all my suggestions is one idea: If we want to enjoy greater states of mental and physical resourcefulness, then we need to script and rehearse our habits with care.

ACT NOW!

I assume that people are malleable. They can change when they choose to wholeheartedly. When I say this, some people respond by saying, "People don't change," or, "You just can't change human nature."

Well, we don't have to worry about something as large and abstract as personality or human nature. That sounds too grand. Instead, we can just concentrate on changing habits one at a time, bit by bit, and enjoying the results in our lives. The notion of changing our act—our habits—is a homely and useful one—simple enough for anyone to grasp yet powerful enough to change our lives.

Changing habits is all an act

Any time you change a habit, eliminate an old one or create a new one, you're acting. As an example, consider a person who almost never smiles. After reading *Act Now*, he becomes convinced of the virtues of smiling and decides to make it a regular part of his life. So one day he marches into his office flashing a smile at everyone in sight. Immediately his surprised coworkers notice and start talking, "Well look at Charlie with the big grin pasted on his face. He's just faking it, you know. It wouldn't be so hard to take if only he'd smile a *real* smile instead."

This response is ironic. His office colleagues have probably said to each other, "Wouldn't it be nice if Charlie would smile and be happy?" Yet when Charlie starts an act that's bound to be amateurish at first, his coworkers complain about insincerity.

Even so, Charlie knows that he has to start his new act sometime, even if it begins as a "bit" part. His colleagues say that his new-found habit of smiling is just an act, and yes, so it is! So what!

Can we expect Charlie to perform it perfectly at first? He is rehearsing, and his supporting cast could just as well applaud his effort. After all, we become what we do.

If we fake a smile often enough, smiling will eventually become a regular part of our facial costume. And when that happens, the smile that once appeared fake becomes the real thing. The interpersonal chemistry that results from his new act will benefit Charlie and the rest of the office players, as well.

It's just fine to fake a new habit. Indeed, how can we change any habit unless we go through a period of faking it? Any new behavior—anything from buckling your seat belt to starting an exercise program—feels awkward and uncomfortable at first. Getting past that initial period of discomfort might take 30 days, six weeks, six months, or even longer.

Patience is important as the new behavior settles into place and starts to feel right. Actors rehearse a new role until the part becomes second nature. Likewise, we can rehearse a new habit until it becomes a part of our standard repertoire, until the chemistry is right!

Perhaps all learning is a matter of acting. If you read psychology texts, you'll often find learning defined as "a permanent change in behavior." That's another way of describing habit change.

Once you accept the need to "fake it 'til you make it," you can use three steps to change any habit: observe, script, and rehearse. I'll describe each step in turn.

ACT NOW!

....

Step 1: Observe your current habits

Changing any habit begins with an act of courage—telling the truth. Before we know which habits to change, we need a base line—an accurate assessment of the way we currently think and behave. It's important to not judge or berate ourselves as we make this assessment. Simply admitting the truth to ourselves and to others unleashes the forces of lasting change.

So, if you want to cut down on coffee but drink eight cups a day, just tell the truth about it. If you swear you're going to exercise on a stationary bike but end up watching *The Simpsons* on television instead, just tell the truth about it. If you promised to give up desserts six weeks ago but consumed five doughnuts last night, just tell the truth about that, too.

Acting students know what it's like to receive criticism of their work. Stanislavski urged each of his students to develop an "understanding critic" on the inside—an ability to mentally stand back and see themselves on stage as a member of the audience would. This calls for playing your part even as you *watch* yourself playing your part.

Enlisting a coach

Sometimes we lack perspective to see our own habits with clarity. For this reason it is often wise for us to find a caring director who can help critique our performance. Finding this person can mean reaching outside our immediate circle of family and friends to a professional counselor. This pays off in an added ability to "look in" to our emotional chemistry.

....

Most of us can't do this alone. And even when we can, we can often benefit from a little coaching.

When critiquing a student, Stanislavski had the wisdom and compassion to first note each student's particular strengths. That's a sound practice for any of us.

As you evaluate and catalog your habits, take some time to affirm what you *are* doing well right now. Notice your habits that are creating happy-healthy chemistry and build on them. Keep building on these healthy pleasures at the same time that you are reconstructing some of the habits you need and want to change. Always accentuate the positive while you eliminate the negative.

So, begin with paying attention to your current habits. To gain focus, concentrate on observing simple things that you say and do daily—for example, the way you walk, your typical posture, the depth and pace of your breathing, and so on.

The aim here is to observe yourself without judging your habits as good or bad. Instead, observe yourself with the cool, detached viewpoint of a scientist in a white lab coat who's simply taking notes on someone else's behavior—no shame, no blame attached.

What you're looking for at this stage is simply to get as much data as you can. Notice the concrete details. You might find that it helps to write down your observations in a journal, log, or chart.

Imagine that your current self-image is a photograph or videotape that's out of focus. You lack a clear picture of what you characteristically do and say. The goal of the attention stage is to bring this image into clear focus with vivid images and a high fidelity sound track.

Step 2: Script new habits

We can follow truth-telling with choice. It's often easier to drop an old habit when we choose to replace it with a new one.

Now that you've captured your habits with a high-resolution image, ask yourself one of the most powerful questions imaginable: "What do I want?"

If your current habits are serving you, then there's probably no need to change them. If you're consistently producing the results in life that you want, then you may not even need this book. The rest of us, however, can imagine new results that we desire. The list is potentially endless: a higher level of health, a higher income, a schedule that's free of hurry and worry, and much more.

Take a few minutes to imagine yourself playing the role you've always wanted to play. In your mind's eye, see yourself moving through an ideal day in the script of your choice—working at the job of your dreams, reaching a new level of health, living in the house and landscape of your choice, seeing the people you'd love to have in your life (your supporting cast). If you notice your excitement and level of enthusiasm rising, then you've accomplished the purpose of this step.

You can gain even more from this step by gathering these fragments of a vision into a coherent whole. Describe your ideal role— both your desired actions and attitudes—in writing. Sketch in a new life script and set of stage directions for the emotional chemistry you'd like to generate every day.

Now that you've created a compelling future for yourself (even if it's just on paper at this point), ask yourself two questions. First, what am I willing to do to enjoy the results I want? In other words, what new habits can make this compelling future a reality? Now you've got the seeds of powerful intention. Write down a list of new habits that will lead you to your goals, including a daily dose of happiness and healthy chemistry.

Think about this step in terms of acting a new role, stepping on to a new stage with new stage direction. Imagine you're an actor preparing to play a new part. Think back to what Stanislavski would say if you were a member of the acting company at the Moscow Art Theater and he was coaching you on stage.

"Above all, remember your super-objective," he would say. "Then think about the through line of actions for your character so you can plot a sure path to the character's supreme goal." If it helps you, translate the term *through line of action* into the more familiar term *habits* and the term *super-objective* into *mission, purpose,* or *goal.*

Say that your objective is to handle money in a healthier way so that it is no longer a source of stress in your life. Then list some simple, concrete changes in your habits to support this objective. For example:

- Eat out only twice each month and put aside the money you save.

- Pay yourself 10 percent first. That is, every time you get a paycheck, immediately deposit 10 percent of that check in your investment account.

- Pay off the balance on your credit cards each month and avoid the high interest charges.

- Find a stable "money director" with whom you are comfortable who will wisely advise and council you on financial matters.

Perhaps you have a medical injury that is compounded by significant pain. And you realize that pain is a subjective feeling modified by many different thoughts and actions. Stanislavski Method acting

ACT NOW!

has taught you that feeling is chemistry, and that chemistry can be changed. As part of "life's audience" you have observed that some people magnify and compound their feelings (chemistry) of pain while others tend to diminish pain's importance. Some can be scripted by others or can script themselves "into" or "out of" pain chemistry. Some turn the pain chemistry higher and some lower it.

Say that your objective is to handle a chronic pain so that it causes less stress in your life. Then list some simple, concrete changes in your habits to support this objective. For example:

- Talk only with your care provider about your pain.

- Don't blame others for your pain. Don't complain to friends or family.

- Avoid people who encourage you to "keep playing" the pain role.

- Remind yourself that only you can "fix" yourself. No one else can fix you.

- Realize that muscle pain is hurtful—not harmful. Move!

- Start "working out" of pain. Begin an exercise routine.

- Connect with society again. Contribute your unique talents. Go to work!

To make your list of habits even more powerful, take a second step. Take a close look at each habit you've listed. What specific change in your action or speech does it call for?

A key word in this stage is *action*. Remember the importance that Stanislavski attached to the "method of physical action." Look for simple, concrete changes in posture, movement, gesture, and speech that are consistent with your super-objective. Make the first word in each habit an active verb: *Eat* more slowly, *walk* each morning, *smile* each time you see your children, *breathe* more slowly when you feel rushed, and so on.

Stanislavski reminded his students that they had to keep three questions in mind at all times to generate effective actions toward their super-objectives: *Why? How?* and *What?* In other words:

- *Why* are you acting? What are your goals in life?

- *How* will you overcome any obstacles to achieving your goal?

- *What* actions (habits) will you take to achieve the goal?

Answering these questions can help us script our thoughts and actions for habits that create the chemical reaction of wealth, health, and happiness.

Step 3: Rehearse without reproach

Review for a minute what you already have in place: a focused picture of your super-objective along with the fire of a steady desire to attain it and a clear vision of the actions (habits) that will lead you to accomplish that objective. All that's left now is to rehearse the part that you've so carefully and thoroughly scripted.

At this point you might find comfort in some other ideas from Stanislavski—that can help you get past common difficulties as you struggle to meet your objectives. First, don't worry about feeling inspired. As Stanislavski said, intangible qualities such as creativity and inspiration are fleeting and undependable. On some days you might feel inspired and truly at one with the part in your script. On others, you might feel completely unmotivated, uninspired, and perfectly willing to settle for your old, familiar part (habits).

ACT NOW!

••

If this happens, you're batting about average. Such ups and downs in motivation are perfectly normal. To get past them, remember that feelings are notoriously impermanent—hardly a reliable guide for action. When feelings of dullness, anger, or fear start to pass over you, simply notice them and accept them. Then focus on your super-objective and chosen habits.

Remember that actions and feelings can function separately, and that it's far easier to directly control your actions than your feelings. You can ride the stationary bike even if you feel tired. You can do a relaxation exercise even if you feel stressed. You can slow down your breathing even when you feel afraid.

In short, when unpleasant feelings arise, *get back to physically playing your part*. As you do, you may find that the feeling chemistry of being stuck changes into the chemistry of genuine inspiration—the beginning of a truly "on" performance in your new role.

Also give some time to mental rehearsal. In your mind's eye, see yourself successfully practicing your new habits, day after day. Often this mental rehearsal will be more effective if you precede it with some deep relaxation (see the instructions for *savasana* on page 181). Then end your rehearsal with an affirmation—a simple, positive statement that you already are the character you wish to be. Some examples are: *I make smiling a regular part of my day. I manage money with ease. I look forward to exercising.*

Finally, rehearse without reproach. During rehearsal, there is no such thing as failure—only mistakes. For added solace, consider the failures that preceded some well-known successes:

• Pablo Picasso left school at age 10 because he was doing so poorly.

• Henry Ford almost flunked out of high school.

••

- Einstein struggled with his early schooling, and one of his teachers recommended that he drop out of high school.

- The first time that Charles Darrow submitted his idea for a new game called *Monopoly*, the Parker Brothers company rejected it because it contained 52 fundamental errors.

- After a successful run of his musical *South Pacific*, composer Oscar Hammerstein took out an ad in *Variety* magazine that listed a number of his productions that flopped. At the bottom of the ad was a line that read, "I did it before, and I can do it again."

In short, you can view mistakes simply as feedback that teach you more about the part you want to play. In life there are many retakes and reenactments required in getting your act together. And when you get the act right, you will be a hard act to follow.

Stanislavski would have said: To establish the right creative state it is essential to work step by step to establish habits. Piecemeal, the habit enters until it (the chemistry) becomes incorporated as second nature. One must constantly rehearse to achieve this true creative chemistry, whether performing in the professional theater or on the stage of life.

ACT NOW!

....

....

SCENE TEN

PERFORM

After you set your stage, costume yourself, script, produce, and rehearse, it's time for your grand performance. You've taken all the steps needed to be a smash hit. Now it's time go on the stage of daily life and steal the show.

While you're at it, have some fun. In this chapter, I suggest some ideas for cultivating laughter, connecting to the other members of your cast, and doing some surprising improvising. Enjoy!

Take a laughter prescription

Laughter is the performance that loosens us up—literally. We often hear that people "crumble with laughter," "go weak with laughter," or "fall to the floor in laughter." Those sayings point to a real physiological effect. A bout of hard laughter triggers the release of endorphins and relaxes tense muscles.

Laughter offers other benefits as well. Norman Cousins (whose story is in scene 1) found that episodes of laughter noticeably reduced his pain during the time he was hospitalized for a near-fatal inflammatory disease. It's possible, as Cousins discovered, for

ACT NOW!

laughter to have an anti-inflammatory effect. What's more, belly laughter simulates the effects of aerobic exercise. After we laugh, our heartbeat and blood pressure decrease—signs of reduced stress. Indeed, laughter is a kind of internal jogging. Finally, the flood of neuropeptides released when you laugh may suppress your appetite. So perhaps there is some wisdom in the old sayings, Live it up," "Lighten up," and "Laugh it off!"

Laughing is one of the easiest and most effective acting techniques to learn. Often I've seen people with chronic aches and pains who forget to laugh for long periods of time. They just don't remember how to access their good feeling chemistries on a regular basis. These people get special instructions from me. I tell them to consciously search out fun and laughter. I ask them to set humor goals: to associate with fun and funny people, go to comedy clubs, read the comics, watch situation comedies on television, and spend more time around young children, who laugh so readily.

I even go so far as to give my patients a laughter prescription. I actually write out a prescription with words to this effect: "Stand in front of the mirror and belly laugh for 15 seconds, three times each day."

What we're talking about here is no ordinary laugh. I mean an all-out, bellowing, no-holds-barred belly laugh. Not just a little twitter but a belly-holding, gut-busting (for some the instructions must be made more graphic), gas-passing guffaw.

Often at the end of a "laughter RX rehearsal" my patients or members of my audiences will have big smiles on their faces—which then suddenly fade. "Oh sure, I can act like this now, but I don't think I can do this at home. My family will laugh at me!"

I reassure them that they are probably right. Their family and friends will laugh at them. But soon most everyone will start laughing *with* them, because there is nothing more contagious and bonding than this prime endorphin-raising activity. We naturally gravitate to people who laugh. When you hear colleagues laughing in a nearby office, you want to be there. We all want to be in on the fun. We want to be connected to the good feeling chemistry that bonds us when we share a laugh.

I've done seminars on the health benefits of laughing with Merrilyn Belgum, a 60-plus-year-old comedian from Fridley, Minnesota. Merrilyn says that in her hometown they don't use such delicate expressions as "laugh 'til you cry" or "laugh 'til you fall down." Instead, they say, "laugh 'til you leak." I apologize if you don't find this funny. But, again, for graphic impact, this is the kind of laughter I'm referring to with the laughter prescription.

Try it right now (the prescription, not the leaking) before reading any further. Just put your book down for a minute and stand right where you are. Now for 15 seconds, laugh as hard as you can. Really let yourself go. Better yet, do this with friends and family members. Go ahead and raise the roof, and don't worry if the roof leaks.

Hard to stop, isn't it? Once you try the laughter prescription, your body will ask you for more. Soon you'll find yourself making time for gut-busting belly laughs at least once a day. Laughter is much like a siphon. Once started it just keeps on going!

After you accept this laughter prescription, take a few moments to analyze the effects. Do you notice any changes in your thinking and your emotional state? Of course you do. You probably find, as I do, that laughter simply feels wonderful. I know of no better way to demonstrate the direct effects of releasing your healing chemistry.

Some people have a hard time a getting into the act of laughing at first. They say, "Well, I tried to laugh and I didn't feel much different." I congratulate them for their effort and ask them to keep it up with their laughter prescription. Continued rehearsal will make all the difference. No actor can get into the chemistry of their part without repeated rehearsals.

Occasionally people will say, "Well, if you want me to laugh, you have to show me something that will *make* me laugh."

"Fine," I reply. "Then I'm going to highlight a line on your laughter prescription, right here under your name, that says 'stand in front of a mirror.'"

Mirrors are great tools for promoting laughter. Just as you smile into the mirror, you can learn to laugh into the mirror. Doing this helps you "reflect" on the most important factor in adding health to your life—you. Where will the chemistry of healing come from in your life, if not from the person looking back at you from the glass?

After some experience with the basic laughter prescription, you're ready for advanced studies. Following are nine steps for healing laughter I give to my top students of humor. Read through these steps a couple of times and then start rehearsing. Better yet, invite another person to join you.

1. To begin, stand in front of a mirror and costume your face. Smile just a bit. At this point, you don't even have to bare any teeth. A subtle smirk will do.

2. Now widen your smile. Open your mouth enough to show a few teeth. Also get your cheeks into the act, perhaps allowing a dimple or two to show.

3. Next, wrinkle your eyes. According to some studies, this modest act begins the release of endorphins. In less scientific terms, I say that a wrinkle adds a twinkle to the eyes. When people are committed to an act of laughter, you see it in their eyes. They light up! You can sense the added spark that begins in and around the eyes.

4. Preserving your toothy grin and the laugh wrinkles around your eyes, wrinkle your forehead as well. If you're doing this exercise with another person, then look at that person. Give him or her the eyebrow wave. Often this is enough to provoke an outburst of laughter.

5. Now add sound. Start laughing and make an effort to generate the sound from your diaphragm instead of your throat. I want you to literally experience a "gut" laugh, so make the sound from your belly. Put your hands on your lower ribs and move the *ha -ho-he* sound toward that area.

6. Next make more sound. Move from *ha* to *ha, ha,* to *ha, ha, ha,* and then to *ha, ha, ha, ha.* Pretend that you're starting a frozen car on a winter morning in Minnesota when the temperature is 20 degrees below zero. You crank the starter and at first you hear only a *ha,* then a *ha, ha.* As the engine continues to warm, put your foot on the accelerator and give it a little gas until you get a roaring *ha, ha, ha, ha, ha, ha, ha, ha, ha!*

7. When you've got your laughter engine hitting on all cylinders, then it's time to get the chassis moving. As you laugh stand up tall, throw your head and shoulders upward, and arch your back. At the same time instruct your body to loosen up and lighten up. Feel all parts of yourself laughing. When your face laughs, your toes laugh!

8. Now get into the act even more. Throw your arms up and back, raising your hands over your head. Wiggle your hands and flap your wings (the scapula bones of the back). You may choose to turn around or add any other movement that feels good.

9. For your grand finale, bring your hands back down and slap your knees or thighs. Keep laughing out loud the whole time. Repeat these three steps as one flowing motion: laugh out loud,

arch backward, then bend forward to slap thighs or knees. As you do, make eye contact with anyone else in the room. Share the laughter with another person or with that person in the mirror. Start a happy-demic!

If you feel awkward with this exercise, remember that's a common reaction. Just accept your feelings and keep rehearsing. I predict that eventually you'll feel so comfortable with this nine-step act that you won't want to stop. Fifteen seconds will hardly seem like enough time.

Commune!

Stanislavski frequently spoke about communion between actors on stage. He pointed to communion as one of the supreme goals of the theater experience and described it in almost mystical terms. According to Stanislavski, we radiate and absorb feelings through our qualities of attention, intention, and action. When actors commune, they enter each other's invisible, inner world and feel with each other. In more modern scientific language we could say they are sharing a similar chemistry.

Communion has a delicate, fragile quality. It is easily lost. When an actor's attention wanders offstage, communion is compromised. The same thing happens when someone forgets her super-objective or acts out of character.

The same principles that help actors commune on stage can help us connect with the key people in our lives. (I prefer the more common term *connect* to *commune*.) We connect with others in many ways—observing, speaking, listening, touching, hugging, massaging, and sexual contact, to name a few.

We connect intellectually when we share others' interests and objectives. We connect with crowds as we root for the home team during a game. We connect spiritually by praying, meditating, and attending a place of worship. We connect with the world through newspapers, magazines, and television. And we connect with animals and plants through contact with nature.

Even the simplest forms of connection can boost our immunity. Some research indicates that pet owners who have surgery get out of the hospital faster than those people who don't have pets. People who have pets want to go home and take care of them. These people feel needed—an excellent argument, I think, for owning pets. In fact, one study indicates that VPs (Vintage People, those over age 65) who own a dog see their physician 16 percent less often than people without dogs. It's a little threatening to me as a physician to think that I can be replaced by a dog!

Dogs have been found to be the most healthful pets for several reasons. People frequently exercise with them. Dogs can be excellent counselors because they're willing to listen almost any time for free. And we pet and groom dogs more than other pets.

In the process of "coming out of ourselves" we connect with others. This helps create the happy-healthy chemistry now being described by scientists. "I" chemistry tends to keep us apart from others, while "we" chemistry tends to bring us into an expanded universe.

Connecting is important in any type of treatment program for chronic illness. Many of the people I've seen with chronic pain are not well connected. Gertie is one example. After retiring, she failed to keep ties with former coworkers. Her family lived some distance away and didn't visit often. She had no close friends and no church or spiritual connection. She belonged to no clubs and didn't volunteer for any community activities. In fact, Gertie lived alone in an

．．

apartment with only a television set for company. Her life was "hurting" and her body manifested her pain.

I suggested that Gertie begin by getting something living in her life by connecting with a pet. However, her apartment owner had strict rules against pets. How about fish? Well, she didn't go for fish. "Then how about plants?" I suggested. "Would you consider raising some plants?"

This idea sparked an interest in Gertie, who began by raising some vines and green plants. Soon there were plants all over her apartment. She was supplying plants to her neighbors—and making new friends. She went to garden shows and garden lectures, which lifted her out of her solitude. Gertie displayed her renewed sense of humor when she related how at a recent flower show she met a "seedy" widowed farmer and she was trying to plant some romantic ideas.

Gertie was fond of repotting plants, something I told her was an exercise in "plant parenthood." Being part of a "growth industry," she started bringing plants into my office. In fact, I have one of Gertie's plants on my desk even as I write this.

After several months I asked her to reflect on her new hobby. "Oh, it's great," she said. "It is challenging. I have something to get up for in the morning. I feel like there is something rooting for me every day. I always wanted to be a plant manager, and now, well, I am one."

Gertie said her favorites were the blooming plants. She went to bed at night and got up in the morning just to look for more blossoms in her apartment. "You know, these plants, all this work I put into them, all this nurturing, and this TLC," she said one day, "well, when one comes into bloom, I can just hear it saying, 'Gertie, this bud's for you!'"

．．

A simple living connection with plants was enough to transform Gertie's attitude toward life. The plants helped take her out of herself and allowed her to share herself again with people and with nature. She had put some living in her life.

In light of this change, imagine how powerful all connections to friends, family, and a spiritual community can be. Most of us readily acknowledge that fact. At the same time, it's common for people to watch months and even years pass without really connecting to the significant people in their lives. This lack is a hollow at the core of life, a feeling of emptiness, a sense that something is missing. That missing something could be better health.

Gertie is just one example of how aches and pains can be diminished and the happy-healthy chemistry produced when someone "branches out." You might say Gertie was a late bloomer. But it's never too late. And incidentally, the "seedy" farmer is now Mr. Gertie.

Each of us needs to set the stage and script specific times to connect with others. Treat these times as you would a business appointment or a trip to your beautician or barber. On your calendar, block out times when you plan to do nothing but see friends, eat a quiet, relaxed dinner with your partner, or visit your children or grandchildren. Also set aside times for your spiritual practice, whatever that may be. Regular attendance at a church, synagogue, or temple, along with prayer or meditation, can increase your sense of being connected.

Healthy actors sometimes improvise by adding movements and even spoken lines that are not in the original script. Stanislavski heartily approved of this practice. One way to achieve inspiration, he said, is to introduce a spontaneous, unexpected incident that is germane to your super-objective and through line of action.

Improvise

Healthy people are often seen as flexible and marked by spontaneous behavior—sudden and surprising intentions that lead to unplanned and yet effective actions.

Stevie Ray, a teacher of improvisational drama, helps individuals understand and experience how acting impacts health, wealth, and happiness. He gives his students a set of imagined circumstances and a goal to attain. With those in mind, the players onstage create their roles on the spot, with no prior scripting. The acting becomes a game, an almost childlike kind of make-believe. Such improvising shows the direct connection between *play* and *playing* a role.

Improvising is what jazz musicians do when they take the stage. When Ray Charles sings "Georgia" or Ella Fitzgerald soars through "How High the Moon," the performance is different every time. These seasoned artists never sing a song the same way twice in a row. They ad-lib, they take chances, they follow the lead of the audience.

In the book *Improvisation for the Theater,* author Viola Spolin says to improvise one must have total trust—in themselves and the rest of the cast.

Improv actors must develop the belief that they or their cast mates can do no wrong. The actors will not say or think "no, but." Instead, they will say, think, and act "yes, and."

The phrase "no, but" reflects the past. "Yes, and" calls forth a future chemistry that helps create a positive "life drama," a chemistry that helps move us toward our goals.

You can do the same on the stage of everyday life. With your super-objective firmly in mind, ask yourself: What can I do today, right now, to bring myself one step closer to my goals? If your answer falls outside your previous plans, so much the better, as long as it works.

When planning, you can allow for the unexpected. Avoid scheduling 100 percent of your time. Regularly leave an hour, an evening, or even a whole day at a time unplanned, and improvise when the time comes. Building in these mini-vacations allows time for connection, laughter, and other essentials of a healing performance.

Give yourself plenty of opportunities to create a "yes, and" chemistry.

ACT NOW!

ENCORE

PREPARE FOR A LONG RUN

It's time to tie up a few loose ends and talk about some potential misunderstandings. Also, I'd like to touch main points once again and suggest which may be the most important for you to remember. Finally, I'll share my hopes for how this book might change your life and offer a "crib sheet" for the happy-healthy act that can turn your chemistry on!

We all act

When I say all of us act, I don't mean we should be shallow or insincere. Rather, I'm pointing out that during the course of daily life we costume, stage, script, produce, direct, rehearse, and perform. And we do all these things in ways that resemble the habits of actors.

Some of my favorite examples of everyday acting are the people in clown clubs—groups that provide volunteer clowns for private parties and community events. Now, suppose you talk to one of these clowns the day of a performance and he says, "Gosh, I feel terrible. It's been a really tough day. And now I have to go off to the children's hospital tonight and act like a clown. I'm afraid I'm not up for this."

ACT NOW!

I'll bet if you talked to this person after the performance, he'd sound like a different person, saying something like, "I didn't feel much like being a clown when I came here tonight. But, you know, the minute I slipped into my costume, I started to feel better. And when I got on stage and heard the laughter of the kids, I couldn't help laughing myself. In just a matter of minutes, I really got into the act. I can't wait to do this again. It's great medicine!"

Actors know they become someone else when they put on a costume. That costume can be anything from a clown outfit or police uniform to a white lab coat or the robes of a priest. I know that I take on a new role when I put on my white coat, don a stethoscope, and enter an examining room to see a patient. When my costume changes, so do I. When in costume I treat patients differently and the patients treat and perceive me differently. To some degree the chemistry has changed in both of us.

Shamans know about the power of costuming for their roles. So do priests, rabbis, ministers, and other religious leaders. For these people, donning a costume is more than a professional obligation; it is a sacred act.

As one minister told me, "When I put on my robe and ascend the pulpit to give a sermon, words are spoken *through* me." When these people shed their sacred costume and have coffee with the parishioners after the service, they are not in the same state of mind. The costume gives them access to new insights and new feelings. Costuming changes their chemistry.

I believe costuming—along with staging, scripting, and the other techniques I've discussed—can change your chemistry, too.

Rewrite your script for aging

If you're a vintage person, a VP, I especially recommend the ideas in *Act Now* to you. Please create your own script for living the years ahead and act as if each day is the first day of the "best" of your life!

In the book *Mindfulness*, Ellen J. Langer, a professor of psychology at Harvard University, describes a study that supports the main themes of *Act Now*. This study "reset the stage" for a group of 75- to 80-year-old men, which led them to a series of physical and psychological benefits.

Researchers began by gathering data on each participant. This included assessments for vision, hearing, stature, gait, strength, muscular flexibility, mental acuity, and overall life satisfaction. Participants were then divided into two groups. Both groups learned they were going to take part in separate, five-day retreats in a rural setting. During these retreats, their main task was to rekindle a past state of mind.

The men in group A, the control group, reminisced with other participants about "the way it was in the old days." At the same time, these men stayed in contact with the "real world." They dined from current menus, read current newspapers, listened to current music, watched current television, and talked about current events. Whenever they talked about the good old days, their script was in the past tense.

Group B totally reenacted the past. For these men, the stage was turned back to 1959. All aspects of their environment—the furnishings, clothing, food, magazines, newspapers, music, and television programming—dated back to that year. Pictures of the participants taken 30 years ago were also displayed. In addition, the men in Group B were asked to "script" their conversation in the *present* tense. These men avoided discussing any events that had taken place since 1959. They aimed to become once again the men they were in 1959—to reincarnate the roles they played 30 years earlier.

Based on photographs and videos completed before and after the retreats, participants in both groups were judged to look three years younger. Both groups showed an improvement in psychological functioning, memory tasks, and hand strength. Both slept and ate better during the retreat than at home. In addition, men in both groups said they felt more in control of their lives during the retreat.

Group B participants, however, enjoyed some further benefits. They showed an additional increase in flexibility, sitting height, manual dexterity, vision, and intelligence.

Dr. Langer draws this conclusion from her study:

> The regular and 'irreversible' cycles of aging that we witness in the later stages of human life may be a product of certain assumptions about how one is supposed to grow old. If we didn't feel compelled to carry out these limiting mind sets, we might have a greater chance of replacing years of decline with years of growth and purpose.

I'd paraphrase Dr. Langer's comments using the language of *Act Now*. The roles we ask people to play during the later scenes of life are based on outdated scripts. If we didn't feel compelled to act from these stereotyped scripts, we could replace some of these "old" roles—roles that have been scripted and overplayed. These old roles of mind-body deterioration that are played so well that the chemistry of the part often becomes a reality.

Dr. Langer and her colleagues demonstrated that we can reverse roles to a degree and play out old age with growth and purpose.

I've seen people in their 30s who complain about getting old. And I've seen others who are 90, 95, or even 100 who say that they still feel young. These "keenagers" forgot to read or refused to read society's script that told them to act decrepit at 60 or 70 or 80.

I'm not saying that people in their 70s or 80s have the physiology of people in their 20s. The aging process brings undeniable changes. But, at the same time, none of us has to script ourselves into a role that calls for aging before our time. If physiologists tell us we have the potential to live to age 120, then why do we say that 65 is the time for us to retire and enjoy our sunset years? Why do we become seniors at this age if we're just entering the mid-point of life? Perhaps, as Dr. Langer notes, aging is more a function of staging than we realize.

Model your mentors

Most of us have role models and mentors. We learn from these people through the techniques of acting—by putting on their "costume" and playing their part. We move the way they move. We dress the way they dress and speak the way they speak. This often happens on a subconscious level. Watch two people who intensely enjoy each other's company. Usually they'll mirror each other's body language—gestures, posture, voice intonation, laughter, and more.

Think of some of our veteran actors, such as George Burns, Bob Hope, or Katharine Hepburn. These people show us by example how to connect, how to contribute to others, and how to script ourselves for a long run. It's no surprise to me that they enjoy relatively good health as well.

The people I've just mentioned are public figures, but no doubt you can name some mentors of your own. I suggest that you adopt a happy-healthy mentor. Be an understudy of someone who's superb at playing a happy-healthful part.

Knowledge evolves

In *Act Now*, I've presented only the barest outlines of a new health paradigm, a new way of thinking about wellness. The overlap between acting and health, between medicine and theater, has barely been explored.

My purpose in this book has not been to prove anything but rather to invite you and my healthcare colleagues to think dramatically. And it's time to encourage the scientific community to develop studies that will measure the techniques of acting on individual and societal well-being.

I'm sure my thinking about health and acting will change as we delve further into this territory. Knowledge and medical practice change constantly, which has lead me to an about-face more than once.

When I graduated from medical school, physicians routinely told patients not to arch their lower backs. Today I tell many people to do back arching exercises regularly. Years ago I also asked my patients to avoid fiber in their diet. Today, if I had a recipe for saw-dust muffins, I would write prescriptions for it.

The moral is people change and so do our thoughts about how to get well and stay well. Effective healing means rewriting our scripts for healing from time to time.

Act ethically

Before ending *Act Now* I must emphasize another key point. As with almost any other body of techniques, acting techniques can be misused. Certainly Hitler was a master of staging, scripting, and costuming. So was Jim Jones, the architect of the Jonestown massacre. Both men knew how to trigger the emotions and alter the feeling chemistry of their audiences. Both left a legacy of death and slavish cult mentality.

Anyone who explores complementary medicines or suggests that acting may be a complementary medicine may be accused of embracing an unscientific alternative medicine. Such accusations are wrong. Embrace? Certainly not! Explore? Yes! This is especially important for us to remember as we look into the health practices and beliefs of other cultures.

Parts of many unconventional alternative medical approaches may have significant benefits that must be explored and quantified. There is a difference between being skeptical with an open mind and being skeptical and hostile with a closed mind. If you look at something with the purpose of discrediting it, then you'll never find the truth.

Joseph Campbell with Bill Moyers in "The Power of Myth" series on PBS said it best: "Those who think they know, know not. And those who know they know not, truly know!"

As we look backstage at Method acting, hopefully we will be able to identify an alternative medicine for the twenty-first century—a complementary medicine that will enhance our healthy chemistry, that will do no harm, and that will reduce healthcare costs.

It's all about choice

I could reduce the theme of this book to one word: *choice*. I urge you to choose your role, your script, your gestures, your postures, and other aspects of your daily performance. My purpose in *Act Now* is to expand our notions about what we can choose, and I use the language of the theater as a means to that end.

The quality of our health hinges on the small and seemingly trivial choices we make scores of times each day. Among them are choices about how to stand, how to breathe, when to smile and laugh, what to wear, what to say, and how to think. The actor's art is to carefully observe these minute-to-minute choices and change them for the purpose of creating a character.

Any of us can acquire this art and use it in the service of our health and happiness. But most of the time we give little attention to the moment-to-moment choices that make up our lives. We run on automatic pilot. We operate almost like robots who think, speak, and move according to someone else's programming. Actors know that they cannot afford to do this. Neither can we. When we start making the small choices with purpose and clarity, we discover a way to transform our emotional states and perhaps alter the chemistry of the human immune system.

By helping actors study and make such choices, Stanislavski created more than a key to memorable theater. He also uncovered a powerful path to health and well-being. Stanislavski's Method unites the discoveries of cognitive psychology and psychoneuroimmunology. Decades before these fields were invented, Stanislavski discovered that the mind and body are one. What's more, he explained how we can use these discoveries in a practical, concrete way. If we want to become well in mind and body, we can take a few tips from Stanislavski and his heirs in the acting community.

Enjoy this new paradigm for health

I hope you've enjoyed reading *Act Now*. I also hope you'll take its spirit to heart and apply some of its suggestions. I invite people working in the medical arts to think dramatically and those in the dramatic arts to think medically. If we can get these two groups working together—if we can bring the paradigm of the stage to the arena of healing—then all of us will benefit.

One of my favorite philosophers is Dr. Seuss. Reading Dr. Seuss has certainly changed my feeling chemistry and that of my family members. I especially enjoyed his last book, titled *Oh The Places You Will Go*. In that book, Dr. Seuss wrote:

Congratulations!

Today is your day.

You're off to Great Places.

You're off and away!

You have brains in your head.

You have feet in your shoes.

You can steer yourself

any direction you choose . . . .

So be sure when you step.

Step with care and great tact

and remember that Life's

a great balancing Act.

ACT NOW!

....

I'd emphasize the last word—*act*. Any of us can act now to release the healing fuels contained within our immune chemistry. These are the fuels that make our performance in life hot and spark the fires of health. I hope that this book will ignite within you a burning desire to learn more about acting. I hope that *Act Now* will help you become a flaming success on the stage of life.

And in the process of getting fired up, I hope you'll make your play performance on this earthly stage one of joy, love, health and happiness. With a turned on chemistry that enables a longer successful run. A critically acclaimed success by all who reviewed it. A smash hit with many encores and much applause. And when the final curtain falls, we all can say, "This was an act well done!"

....

APPENDIX

The healthy actor's crib sheet

This list contains acting tips to turn up and on the chemistry of happiness and health. The endorphins, morphine-like in structure, are some of the psychoneuroimmune chemicals that enhance our well-being. They have been described as the inner uppers that get us high on life. So come on, live it up, and act well. Role with it. Act now!

The Happy Role

Thoughts—Think Up

—You focus on thoughts that are upward, outward, forward, changing, exploring, opening.

—You think in terms of we, us, and you, rather than I. You connect with others; you do onto others

—You center on happy, positive, glad, and sensual thinking.

—You tell yourself you are a "part of," not "apart from."

ACT NOW!

Face—Look Up

—Your eyebrows arch up. Your expression is open, sparkling.

—Your mouth is up-turned in a smile.

—Your expressions are mobile, fluid, changing.

Body—Stand Up

—Your body is open to expand, arch up, move with grace.

—You are stable, balanced, strong, sure.

Motion—Open Up

—You are able to broaden, widen, roll outward and upward, as expressed through your head, neck, shoulders, back, arms, legs, hand movements.

—Your appear to always be advancing forward.

Voice—Speak Up

— Your voice is energetic, pleasantly pitched, confident but not strident.

—Your speaking has a musical quality, reflected in tone, rhythm, and tempo.

Breathing—Puff Up

—Your breathing is deep, slow, and steady.

Eyes—Brighten Up

—Your eyes are wide open, searching, focused.

—Your eyes make contact with others.

Costume—Dress Up

—You dress in costumes that are appropriate, stylish, well-tailored, and colorful.

Hygiene—Clean Up

—You take good care of your body so you reflect an image that is well groomed, clean, tastefully fragrant, and pleasant to look at.

Skin—Shine Up

—You do what you can to make sure your skin is warm, moist, and smooth.

Music—Tune Up

—You choose up-beat music.

Stage—Set Up

—You plan and arrange your environment with happy props.

Cast—Team Up

—You choose a friendly, successful supporting cast.

ACT NOW!

· ·

Color—Tone up

—You choose colors that turn you on.

Taste—Eat Up

—You dish up foods that evoke happy feelings.

Aroma—Smell Up

—You choose aromas that evoke happy memories.

· ·

BIBLIOGRAPHY

Campbell, Joseph with Bill Moyers. *The Power of Myth*, New York: Doubleday, 1988.

Chesterman, Robert, ed. *Conversations with Conductors*, Totowa, NJ: Rowman and Littlefield, 1976.

Chopra, Deepak. *Ageless Body, Timeless Mind*, New York: Harmony, 1993.

Cousins, Norman. *Anatomy of an Illness as Perceived by the Patient*, New York, NY: Bantam, 1979.

———*The Healing Heart: Antidotes to Panic and Helplessness*, New York: Norton, 1983.

——— *Head First: The Biology of Hope*, New York: Dutton, 1989.

Covey, Steven R. *The Seven Habits of Highly Effective People*, New York: Fireside, 1989.

Davis, Joel. *Endorphins: New Waves in Brain Chemistry*, Garden City, NY: Dial, 1984.

Frankl, Viktor. *Man's Search for Meaning: An Introduction to Logotherapy*, New York: Washington Square, 1959.

Halpern, Steven, with Louis Savary. *Sound Health: Music and*

 **ACT NOW!**

Sounds That Make Us Whole, San Francisco: Harper and Row, 1985.

Kabat-Zinn, Jon. *Full Catastrophe Living: Using the Wisdom of Your Body and Mind to Face Stress, Pain and Illness*, Delta, 1990.

Langer, Ellen J. *Mindfulness*, Reading, Mass.: Addison-Wesley, 1989.

Locke, Steven and Douglas Colligan. *The Healer Within: The New Medicine of Mind and Body*, New York: Dutton, 1986.

Moore, Sonia. T*he Stanislavski System: The Professional Training of an Actor*. New York: Penguin, 1960.

Moyers, Bill. *Healing and the Mind*, New York: Doubleday, 1993.

Murphy, Michael. *The Future of the Body*, Los Angeles: Tarcher, 1992.

Nhat Hanh, Thich. *The Miracle of Mindfulness: A Manual on Meditation*, Boston: Beacon, 1976.

Ornstein, Robert and David Sobel. *The Healing Brain*, New York: Simon and Schuster, 1987.

———*Healthy Pleasures*, Reading, MA: Addison-Wesley, 1989.

Padus, Emrika, ed. *The Complete Guide to Your Emotions & Your Health: New Dimensions in Mind/Body Healing*, Emmaus, PA: Rodale Press, 1986.

Reynolds, David K. *Constructive Living*. Honolulu: University of Hawaii, 1984.

Spolin, Viola. *Improvisation for the Theater*. Evanston, IL: Northwestern University Press, 1963.

Stanislavski, Constantin. *An Actor Prepares*, New York: Theatre Arts Books, 1936.

Waitley, Denis. *The Winner's Edge*, New York: Times Books, 1980.

Ziglar, Zig. *See You at the Top*, Gretna, LA: Pelican, 1979.

Discography

The following list includes names of artists, compositions, and recordings you may find useful for relaxing and enjoying a healing feeling. This is not an exhaustive list—only a place to start if you're looking for ideas. In keeping with the spirit of open-mindedness, these suggestions are listed alphabetically without regard to category or type of music. Choose what works for you. Many of them are available at your local library.

Bach, Johann Sebastian
> *Concerto in G Minor for Flute and Strings*
> *Mass in B Minor*
> *Ayre on a G-String*
> *The Well-Tempered Clavier*

Corelli, Arcangelo
> *Concerto No. 7 in D Minor*
> *Concerto No. 8 in D Minor*
> *Concerto No. 9 in A Major*
> *Concerto No. 10 in F Major*

ACT NOW!

Halpern, Steven
>   *Dawn*

Handel, George Frideric
>   *Concerto No. 1 in B-Flat Major*
>   *Concerto No. 1 in F*
>   *Concerto No. 3 in D*

Holst, Gustav
>   *The Planets*

Horn, Paul
>   *Inside*

Kitaro
>   *Silk Road*

Lynch, Ray
>   *Deep Breakfast*
>   *No Blue Thing*

Stearns, Michael
>   *Morning Jewel*

Tchaikovsky, Peter Ilich
>   *Piano Concerto in B Minor*

Telemann, Georg Philipp
> *Concerto in G Major*

Vivaldi, Antonio
> *Concerto in C Major for Mandolin, Strings, and Harpsichord*
> *Concerto in D Major for Guitar and Strings*
> *Concerto in D Minor for Viola d'Amore*
> *Concerto in F Major*
> *The Four Seasons*

Windham Hill

See the series of Windham Hill "sampler" recordings, anthologies of recordings by various artists, released annually. These may lead you to individual artists you like.

Winston, George
> *Autumn*

Winter, Paul
> *Common Ground*

ACT NOW!

....

....

INDEX

●●●

●●●

ABOUT THE AUTHOR

Dale L. Anderson, M.D., has been a physician for over 35 years. He has practiced as a family doctor, a board-certified surgeon, and a board-certified emergency physician. Dr. Anderson has been an associate director of clinical research for two Fortune 500 Companies and medical director of three of the Twin Cities' largest emergency departments.

His current practice is in the "Complementary Care Department of Park Nicollet Clinic, one of the country's largest multispecialty clinics.

Dr. Anderson is a member of the American Medical Association, the Minnesota Medical Association, and the Ramsey County Medical Society and is a Fellow in the American College of Surgeons. He is also part of the American Association of Therapeutic Humor, the Medical Speakers Association, the National Speakers Association, the Minnesota Speakers Association and the Physicians in Public Broadcast Association.

Through his speaking company, J'ARM Inc., Dr. Anderson performs internationally as a keynote speaker and seminar leader (over 125 per year). Among his colleagues in both the speaking and medical profession, he is recognized as one of America's leading health "edu-tainers."

ACT NOW!

His book *Muscle Pain Relief in 90 Seconds: The Fold and Hold Method,* also published by Chronimed Publishing, has been described as the common sense approach to mastering Mother Nature's mobilization techniques that often erase common muscular aches and pains overnight.

CHRONIMED PUBLISHING
BOOKS OF RELATED INTEREST

Muscle Pain Relief in 90 Seconds by Dale Anderson, M.D. Now you're only 90 seconds away from relieving your muscle pain—drug free! From back pain and shin splints to headaches and tennis elbow, Dr. Anderson's innovative "Fold and Hold" technique can help. Simple, safe, and painless, this method is a must for all of us with muscle aches and twinges.

004257   ISBN 1-56561-058-X $10.95   ❏

Taking the Work Out of Working Out by Charles Roy Schroeder, Ph.D. This breakthrough guide shows how to easily convert what many consider to be a chore into enjoyable, creative, and sensual experiences that you'll look forward to. Includes methods for every form of exercise—including aerobics, weight lifting, jogging, dance, and more!
•A Doubleday Health Book Club Selection

004246   ISBN 1-56561-049-0 $9.95   ❏

The Business Traveler's Guide to Good Health on the Road edited by Karl Neumann, M.D., and Maury Rosenbaum. This innovative guide shows business travelers how to make smart food choices, exercise in planes, trains, automobiles, and hotel rooms, relieve stress, and more. Plus, this guide has a listing of hotels in the U.S. and Canada with fitness facilities. All this, presented with a generous seasoning of fun and interesting facts and tidbits, makes the book a must for every business traveler's expense list.

004233   ISBN 1-56561-036-9 $12.95   ❏

Fight Fat and Win, Updated & Revised Edition by Elaine Moquette-Magee, R.D., M.P.H. This breakthrough book explains how to easily incorporate low-fat dietary guidelines into every modern eating experience, from fast food and common restaurants to quick meals at home, simply by making smarter choices.

004244   ISBN 1-56561-047-4 $9.95   ❏

Fight Fat & Win Cookbook by Elaine Moquette-Magee, M.P.H., R.D. Now you can give up fat and create great tasting foods without giving up your busy lifestyle. Born from the bestseller *Fight Fat & Win*, this practical cookbook shows you how to make more than 150 easy and tempting snacks, breakfasts, lunches, dinners, and desserts that your family will never know contain little or no fat.

004254   ISBN 1-56561-055-5 $12.95   ❏

Fast Food Facts, Revised and Expanded Edition by Marion Franz, R.D., M.S. This revised and up-to-date best-seller shows how to make smart nutrition choices at fast food restaurants—and tells what to avoid. Includes complete nutrition information of more than 1,500 menu offerings from the 37 largest fast food chains.

Standard-size edition, 004240	ISBN 1-56561-043-1	$7.95	❏
Pocket edition, 004228	ISBN 1-56561-031-8	$4.95	❏

Convenience Food Facts by Arlene Monk, R.D., C.D.E., with an introduction by Marion Franz, R.D., M.S. Includes complete nutrition information, tips, and exchange values on more than 1,500 popular name brand processed foods commonly found in grocery store freezers and shelves. Helps you plan easy-to-prepare, nutritious meals.

004081	ISBN 0-937721-77-8	$10.95	❏

The Brand-Name Guide to Low-Fat and Fat-Free Foods by J. Michael Lapchick with Rosa Mo, R.D., Ed.D. For the first time in one easy-to-swallow guide is a compendium of just about every brand-name food available containing little or no fat—with complete nutrition information.

004242	ISBN 1-56561-045-8	$9.95	❏

The Healthy Eater's Guide to Family & Chain Restaurants by Hope S. Warshaw, M.M.Sc., R.D. Here's the only guide that tells you how to eat healthier in over 100 of America's most popular family and chain restaurants. It offers complete and up-to-date nutrition information and suggests which items to choose and avoid.

004214	ISBN 1-56561-017-2	$9.95	❏

Fat Is Not a Four-Letter Word by Charles Roy Schroeder, Ph.D. Through interesting scientific, nutritional, and historical evidence, this controversial and insightful guide shows why millions of "overweight" people are unnecessarily knocking themselves out to look like fashion models. It offers a realistic approach to healthful dieting and exercise.

004095	ISBN 1-56561-000-8	$14.95	❏

Exchanges for All Occasions by Marion Franz, R.D., M.S. Exchanges and meal planning suggestions for just about any occasion, sample meal plans, special tips for people with diabetes, and more.

004201	ISBN 1-56561-005-9	$12.95	❏

366 Low-Fat Brand-Name Recipes in Minutes by M.J. Smith, M.S., R.D./L.D. Here's more than a year's worth of the fastest family favorites using the country's most popular brand-name foods—from Minute Rice® to Ore Ida®—while reducing unwanted calories, fat, salt, and cholesterol.

004247	ISBN 1-56561-050-4	$12.95	❏

All-American Low-Fat Meals in Minutes by M.J. Smith R.D., L.D., M.A. Filled with tantalizing recipes and valuable tips, this cookbook makes great-tasting low-fat foods a snap for holidays, special occasions, or everyday. Most recipes take only minutes to prepare.

004079   ISBN 0-937721-73-5 $12.95 ❑

60 Days of Low-Fat, Low-Cost Meals in Minutes by M.J. Smith, R.D., L.D., M.A. Following the path of the best-seller *All American Low-Fat Meals in Minutes*, here are more than 150 quick and sumptuous recipes complete with the latest exchange values and nutrition facts for lowering calories, fat, salt, and cholesterol. This book contains complete menus for 60 days and recipes that use only ingredients found in virtually any grocery store—most for a total cost of less than $10.

004205   ISBN 1-56561-010-5 $12.95 ❑

Beyond Alfalfa Sprouts & Cheese: The Healthy Meatless Cookbook by Judy Gilliard and Joy Kirkpatrick, R.D., includes creative and savory meatless dishes using ingredients found in just about every grocery store. It also contains helpful cooking tips, complete nutrition information, and the latest exchange values.

004218   ISBN 1-56561-020-2 $12.95 ❑

One Year of Healthy, Hearty, & Simple One-Dish Meals by Pam Spaude and Jan Owan-McMenamin, R.D., is a collection of 365 easy-to-make healthy and tasty family favorites and unique creations that are meals in themselves. Most of the dishes take under 30 minutes to prepare.

004217   ISBN 1-56561-019-9 $12.95 ❑

Foods to Stay Vibrant, Young & Healthy by Audrey C. Wright, M.S., R.D., Sandra K. Nissenberg, M.S., R.D., and Betsy Manis, R.D. From tips on increasing bone strength to losing weight, here's everything women in midlife need to know to keep young and healthy through food. With authoritative advice from three of the country's leading registered dietitians, women over 40 can eat their way to good health and feel better than ever!

004256   ISBN 1-56561-057-1 $11.95 ❑

200 Kid-Tested Ways to Lower the Fat in Your Child's Favorite Foods by Elaine Moquette-Magee, M.P.H., R.D. For the first time ever, here's a much needed and asked for guide that gives easy, step-by-step instructions to cutting the fat in the most popular brand-name and homemade foods kids eat every day—without them even noticing.

004231   ISBN 1-56561-034-2 $12.95 ❑

Chronimed Publishing
P.O. Box 59032
Minneapolis, Minnesota 55459-9686

Place a check mark next to the book(s) you would like sent. Enclosed is
$ _____. (Please add $3.00 to this order to cover postage and handling. Minnesota residents add 6.5% sales tax.)

Send check or money order, no cash or C.O.D.'s. Prices and availability are subject to change without notice.

Name_____

Address_____

City _____State _____Zip_____

Allow 4 to 6 weeks for delivery.

Quantity discounts available upon request.

Or order by phone: 1-800-848-2793,

612-546-1146 (Minneapolis/St. Paul metro area).

Please have your credit card number ready.